First published in Great Britain in 2013
Bloomsbury Publishing Plc
50 Bedford Square
London WC1B 3DP
www.bloomsbury.com

ISBN 978-1-4081-9193-4

Copyright © RotoVision SA 2013

CIP Catalogue records for this book are available from the British Library and
the US Library of Congress.

Editor: Liz Jones
Commissioning Editor: Isheeta Mustafi
Art Editor: Jennifer Osborne
Art Director: Emily Portnoi
Design and illustration: Natalie Clay
Technical Adviser: Sara Cook, Brighton Fashion and Textile School
and Joanna Corney
Photography: Michael Wicks
Picture research: Diane Leyman
Cover Design: Emily Portnoi
Cover image: Handquilted Modern Meadow Picnic Throw by Joel Dewberry

Printed in China

Quiltessential

A VISUAL DIRECTORY OF CONTEMPORARY PATTERNS, FABRICS & COLOUR

ERIN BURKE HARRIS

BLOOMSBURY

LONDON · NEW DELHI · NEW YORK · SYDNEY

CONTENTS

INTRODUCTION

I vividly remember being 10 years old and absolutely fascinated that my 14-year-old cousin had a sewing machine and could make things. I watched her cut the fabric, pin it together and sew the seams – entranced the entire time. I knew right then that I wanted to learn to sew. Three years later, when the opportunity presented itself, along with a lot of urging from my mother, I took home economics in the seventh grade. I've been sewing ever since.

Quilting entered my life relatively recently. Amazed and inspired by the variety of contemporary quilts I was seeing on the Internet, I jumped right in. I knew little to nothing about quilting except that the seams should be 6 mm (¼ in). Confident in my sewing ability, but lacking any real quilting knowledge, I started a quilt for a double bed. As naïve as I was about quilting, I learned a lot working on that first quilt project, especially from the mistakes I made along the way. As frustrating as those errors were, I successfully finished the quilt and started on the next one. Again, I was hooked.

Making a quilt can seem like a daunting prospect, but it is really quite simple. Anyone who has the will to make a quilt and is armed with a little know-how can do this. My goal with this book is to help you get from the idea of a quilt to the reality of it. I have compiled information on the multiple aspects of quilting and put it together in this reference manual that will have you designing and constructing your own quilts in no time at all.

While the book does not include specific quilting projects, I cover all the basics you need to think about when making a quilt. From what fabrics to use, how to develop your colour palette and different quilting styles and designs, to ways to piece and assemble the layers – it's all here. I've also interviewed a handful of talented contemporary quilters whose work will inspire you creatively to keep sewing and to keep quilting.

Quiltessential will give you the information and the confidence you need to create your own project from start to finish. It's my sincere hope that it will also inspire you to make quilts that will be treasured for years to come.

Erin Burke Harris

QUILTING TOOLS

The tools on these pages should get you started. You can then gradually add to your toolkit as you work through different projects.

SCISSORS

You'll need one pair of scissors for cutting fabric – 20 cm (8 in) dressmaker's shears are a good choice. A second pair of scissors should be used when cutting paper patterns, plastic templates and the like. Embroidery scissors or small snips are helpful for trimming threads close to the fabric.

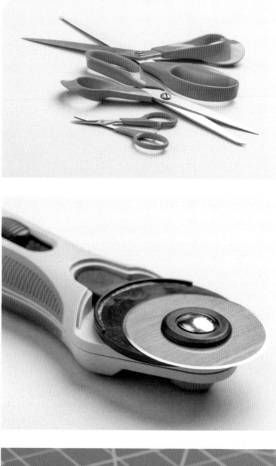

ROTARY CUTTER

While quilting fabric can certainly be cut with scissors, using a rotary cutter is faster and more efficient. These tools have extremely sharp blades, which makes slicing through fabric easy, but care is required when using them. Dull blades should be replaced promptly to avoid injury.

Rotary cutters are available in a wide range of styles, all with different handles and safety mechanisms. They also come with blades ranging in size from 18 mm to 60 mm, with 45 mm being the most common. Larger blades are for more utilitarian cutting, while smaller blades work well on curves and little pieces.

SELF-HEALING CUTTING MAT

These gridded cutting mats are necessary when cutting fabric using a rotary cutter. A 61 × 91 cm (24 × 36 in) mat is a good choice to start with – it will allow you plenty of room to cut large pieces of fabric, but isn't so large that it won't fit on a small table. Smaller mats are helpful for travelling to classes, but larger sizes are wonderful if you have the table space to accommodate them.

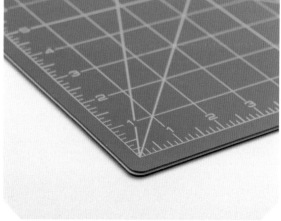

ACRYLIC QUILTER'S RULERS

Also essential for rotary cutting fabric, quilter's rulers are manufactured in myriad shapes and sizes. These gridded rulers are clear acrylic, which allows you to see through them and line up the fabric for cutting. The most basic and useful size is a 15 × 61 cm (6 × 24 in) rectangular ruler, which can be used for almost all your cutting needs. Over time you are likely to accumulate a collection of different quilting rulers. Square rulers of different sizes are helpful when squaring up blocks, and other speciality shapes may be useful for particular patterns.

PINS

Straight pins are essential for piecing. Sharp, thin pins with glass heads will easily pierce the fabric without leaving a large hole and can be ironed without fear of them melting. Store them in a pincushion and replace them when they become dull. Quilter's safety pins are needed for pin tacking. Their curved side allows you to easily manoeuvre them through all layers of the quilt sandwich and back to the top.

IRON AND IRONING BOARD

A steam iron with multiple heat settings is crucial for ironing wrinkles from fabrics and pressing seams. A standing ironing board works well for all ironing purposes. Table-top and space-saving versions are great for small workspaces.

SEWING MACHINE

Any machine with straight and zig-zag stitches and good tension will work for piecing a quilt. If you plan on machine quilting your projects, look for a machine that can accommodate a walking foot and has free-motion capability. A 6 mm (¼ in) patchwork presser foot is extremely helpful.

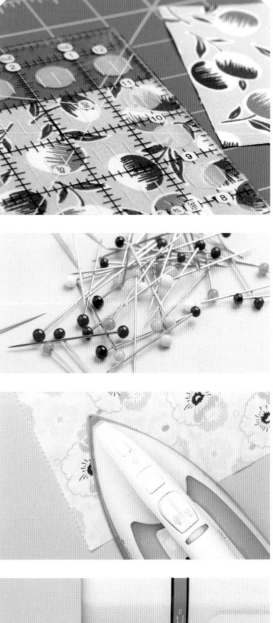

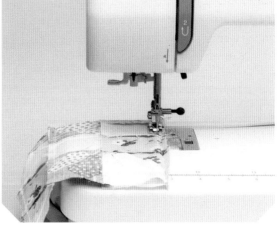

SEWING NEEDLES

Universal machine needles in sizes 75/11 or 80/12 are suitable for piecing most quilting cottons. Heavier fabrics and different fibres may require speciality needles. Remember to replace your machine needles frequently – a good rule of thumb is to use a new needle for each new project.

For hand sewing, quilters often use sharps and betweens. Sharps are medium length with a sharp point and are used for general hand sewing. Betweens are shorter than sharps and are often used for hand quilting because their short length allows for quick, small stitches. Both come in a variety of sizes – the larger the number, the smaller the needle.

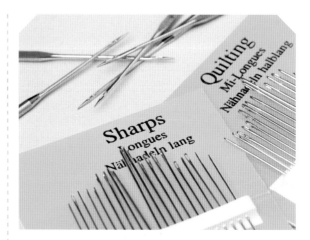

THREAD

For quilting and piecing cotton fabrics, high-quality, 100-per cent cotton thread is recommended. 50 wt is the most common weight, but threads with heavier and lighter counts can be used as well. The smaller the number weight, the heavier the thread is. Fabrics manufactured from other fibres may work better with a silk, rayon or polyester thread.

SEAM RIPPER

As unfortunate as it may be, sometimes stitches newed to be removed. Therefore, a good seam ripper is necessary. It will help unpick stitches efficiently and easily.

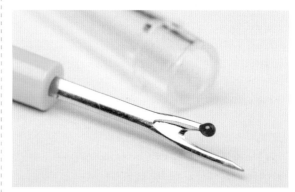

MEASURING TAPE

Any good sewing kit, quilting or otherwise, should contain a measuring tape. Longer than a quilting ruler, this tool is handy for measuring large expanses of fabric as well as finished quilts.

MARKING PENS AND PENCILS

To trace templates and mark quilting patterns, you'll need a variety of marking tools. Different types of marking pens and pencils are available in different colours and thicknesses. Water-soluble disappearing ink, tailor's chalk and a basic HB pencil are useful for quilters.

SPRAY STARCH

Applying starch to fabrics makes it easy to cut and gives the fabric a more paper-like feel. It is especially helpful when piecing small shapes and sewing bias edges.

SKETCHBOOK AND COLOURED PENCILS/MARKERS

Having a place to jot down inspirations, notes and specifics for different quilts is indispensable. Keeping a sketchbook close is wonderful for sketching design ideas and working out the mechanics of a particular quilt pattern.

TEMPLATE PLASTIC

Frosted, lightweight plastic for making templates of pattern pieces is available at quilting stores. It is easy to cut with scissors and can be seen through, which may be helpful for placement on the fabric. Heavyweight card will also work if need be.

BLUE PAINTER'S TAPE

This low-tack masking tape is perfect for taping down fabric without having to worry about ruining floors and table surfaces. It is also convenient when machine quilting to use as a guide for straight quilting lines.

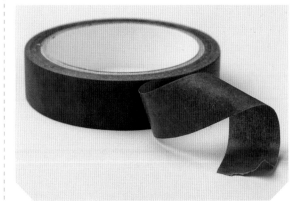

1

SECTION ONE
FABRICS

✾ 1: TYPES OF FABRICS

A beautiful quilt begins with beautiful fabric, and the range contemporary quilters have to select from is seemingly endless. Although quilting cotton is the classic choice, other cotton substrates and textiles made from linen, silk and wool are also being used in quilts today. Armed with a little knowledge, you'll be confident in your fabric choices for your next project.

 # QUILTING COTTON

When it comes to making quilts, cotton is the go-to fabric. Quilting cottons are easy to find and cover a wide range of colours and styles. Full lines of coordinating prints are released a few times each year, giving quilters a plethora of options to choose from.

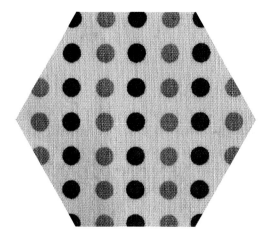

CHARACTERISTICS

Quilting cotton is a good-quality woven fabric that has a tight, even weave without slurs and broken threads. It has a higher thread count than many other woven cottons and its lightweight, smooth texture makes it ideal for quilting.

PROS

Quilting cotton is strong and will wear well over a long period of time. It is less expensive than other fibres and is readily available at large fabric stores and specialist quilt shops. Quilting cotton takes colour well and is manufactured in a variety of patterns and solid colours. Easy to cut and sew, this fabric handles well.

CONS

Depending on the type of dye used to colour the base cloth, some dark and saturated colours may bleed. Cottons shrink and wrinkle easily so the fabric must be pressed before use.

SUITABLE APPLICATIONS

Almost any quilt can be constructed with quilting cotton. It holds a good crease, making it ideal for all piecing methods, as well as hand and machine sewing.

SEWING TIPS

Sew with a universal needle and a good-quality cotton or polycotton thread using a regular presser foot. A hot steam iron is essential for pressing seams.

CARE TIPS

It's a good idea to pre-wash quilting cotton, but it can also be used straight off the bolt. A cold to warm water wash with a low tumble dry is usually sufficient for cotton, but double-check the bolt for specific care instructions. If you skip the pre-wash, take shrinkage into consideration when calculating your fabric requirements.

MUSLIN

Muslin originated in the Middle East and made its way to Europe via India. It has a wide range of uses and is a welcome addition to any quilter's stash.

CHARACTERISTICS

Quilting muslin is a loosely woven, inexpensive cotton fabric that is natural or white in colour. It is soft and plain with slightly irregular yarns across an even weave. Readily available and generally inexpensive, muslin is manufactured in a variety of weights with varying quality. Smooth, high-quality muslins are preferred by most quilters.

PROS

Muslin is less expensive than quilting cotton and is readily available at fabric and quilt stores. It takes dye well and is often available prepared for dyeing (PFD).

CONS

Not all muslins are created equal, and lower-quality muslins may be coarse and somewhat transparent. Also, its looser weave and lower thread count means that it may shrink more than quilting cotton.

SUITABLE APPLICATIONS

Muslin is used as a lightweight foundation when string piecing or as a stabilising fabric. As it is often available in wider widths, muslin can make a nice quilt backing. Bleached muslin is a good choice for white sashing and borders. Muslin is also easily hand and machine sewn, making it extremely versatile for most quilting applications.

✿ BROADCLOTH

Originally produced in wool, today's broadcloths are also made from silk, cotton or a cotton-polyester blend. For quilting, the cotton and cotton-polyester blends are used most often.

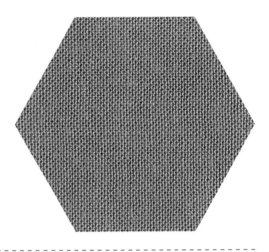

CHARACTERISTICS
Broadcloth is a woven fabric that is characterised by a plain weave with a crosswise rib. It has a smooth finish and a slight sheen. As it is heavier than quilting cotton, cotton broadcloth has a tighter weave.

PROS
Broadcloths are sturdy and stand up to heavy use, making them a good choice for utility quilts. Available in a wide range of solid colours, they are often less expensive than quilting cottons.

CONS
The tighter weave and heavier hand of broadcloths make them difficult for hand piecing and quilting. Cotton-polyester blends pill easily and do not wear as well as cotton broadcloths. They also melt when pressed with a hot iron and are not recommended when sewing quilts.

SUITABLE APPLICATIONS
Solid coloured cotton broadcloths make wonderful quilt backings, sashings and borders. Because they can be heavier than quilting cottons, take care when piecing the two types of fabric in the same project.

SEWING TIPS
Machine sewing and quilting are recommended when using broadcloth. A universal needle with a slightly longer stitch length will be sufficient for the tight weave.

CARE TIPS
As with all cottons, shrinkage will occur when broadcloth is laundered. Pre-wash or increase your fabric quantity to take shrinkage into consideration. Use a hot steam iron to press seams and wrinkles.

 # VOILE

Many contemporary fabric designers are printing their designs on substrates other than quilting cotton, and voile is one of these. With the variety and number of prints increasingly available, this lightweight cotton fabric is gaining popularity among quilters because of its soft, silky feel.

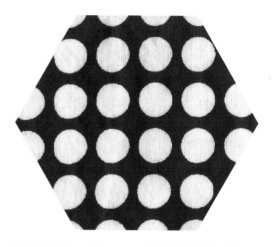

CHARACTERISTICS

Voile is a woven cotton fabric with a beautiful drape. Often used to sew blouses and dresses, it is light in weight and somewhat sheer with a smooth, soft hand. Because it takes dye well, it is available in an increasing range of vivid prints and solid colours.

PROS

Like cotton lawn, voile is suited to almost all piecing and quilting methods. Lighter than quilting cotton, it is good for foundation piecing and warmer-climate quilts. Its wider width makes it a good choice for quilt backs as well.

CONS

Because voile has a silky finish, it can be slippery and hard to work with. Dense quilting can make voile stiff.

SEWING TIPS

Use sharp pins and a new, small needle when working with voile to produce the smallest holes possible. A walking foot, quilt gloves and ample tacking can all protect the fabric from slipping.

CARE TIPS

Voile can be machine washed and dried, but it will shrink.

 LAWN

This luxurious fabric gets its name from Laon, France, where it was first manufactured. Primarily an apparel fabric, lawn can also be used in quilts. The most well-known lawn is produced by Liberty of London in its trademark floral patterns.

CHARACTERISTICS
Lawn is a plain, even-weave fabric that is semi-sheer with a slight sheen. It was originally made from linen, but is now readily available in cotton. The smooth finish and soft hand of lawn give it a beautiful drape and make it a wonderful choice for quilting projects.

PROS
Because it is a lightweight fabric, lawn does not produce bulky seams and works wonderfully with foundation and string piecing techniques. It is available in a variety of prints and solid colours. When paired with a low-loft wadding, it makes for a soft, summer-weight quilt that can be easily machine or hand quilted.

CONS
Lawn is more expensive than and not as widely available as quilting cottons.

CARE TIPS
Cotton lawns shrink and fray. It's best to pre-wash them in the same manner in which you will launder your quilt.

 # CALICO

In the UK, calico is often a simple, inexpensive fabric in white or unbleached cotton, which is referred to as muslin in the US. For quilting purposes, the US definitions of calico (described below) and muslin are more common.

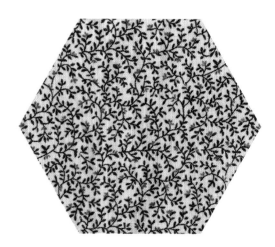

CHARACTERISTICS

A tightly woven cotton fabric, calico features an all-over, repeating print that is generally small in scale. Usually these floral and geometric patterns are just a few colours on a contrasting colour background. Contemporary use of calico often refers to the type of print, not the fabric itself.

PROS

This is easy to find and is a traditional quilting fabric.

CONS

The pattern is printed on one side of the fabric only. Because some calicoes are printed with resists, the colours may run due to discharge dyes.

SUITABLE APPLICATIONS

Calico is good to use in any piecing or quilting method. The traditional style of the calico prints makes it a good choice for patchwork.

CARE TIPS

Bleed test calico to check for running colours. Pre-wash the fabric or allow extra fabric to accommodate shrinkage.

 FLANNEL

Nothing is quite as comforting as snuggling up under a soft, cosy quilt – especially if that quilt is made from flannel.

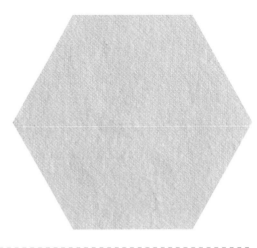

CHARACTERISTICS
Flannel is soft, brushed cotton with a light weave and a nap. Durable, yet comfy and cosy, flannel is readily available in solid colours and prints.

PROS
Due to its cuddly and tactile nature, flannel makes extremely cosy quilts and is a great fabric choice when quilting for babies. Flannel quilts look great when tied, but are also very easily machine sewn and quilted.

CONS
Most flannel shrinks more than quilting cotton. Because it stretches easily, take care when cutting flannel on the bias. It can be difficult to hand sew and quilt, so it's best to stick to the sewing machine.

SEWING TIPS
Applying spray starch to flannel will make it easier to cut. To reduce stretching when sewing, use a walking foot and many pins. Flannel can dull needles faster than other fibres, so start your quilt with a new needle and change it frequently. Because it sheds extra fibres flannel has a tendency to fuzz up the sewing machine, so clean your machine often.

CARE TIPS
Flannel shrinks up to 5 per cent, and different flannels will shrink at different rates, so pre-washing is a good idea.

 # LINEN

Prized for its soft hand and cool feel, this classic fabric is a wonderful choice for patchwork quilts. Combined with other fibres or on its own, linen makes beautiful, cosy quilts. Many companies are also manufacturing cotton-linen blends in bright, contemporary prints and beautiful, solid colours that are perfect for quilting. These fabrics have the look and feel of linen, with a price tag much closer to cotton.

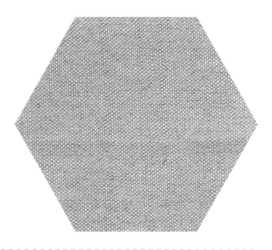

CHARACTERISTICS

Made from the fibres of the flax plant, linen is a woven textile with a crisp texture. Available in many different weights, it is extremely breathable and cool in warm climates.

PROS

This natural fibre takes dye well and can be found in many different solid colours. More textured than quilting cotton, linen feels good to the touch and softens with each laundering.

CONS

Linen shrinks substantially and wrinkles easily. Due to the time-consuming process of producing this textile, linen can also be costly, especially when compared with cotton.

SEWING TIPS

Linen has a tendency to fray and stretch. Handle it as little as possible, cut with the grain and use spray starch to stabilise the fabric. Increase the seam allowance when sewing loosely woven linen.

CARE TIPS

Linen will shrink when laundered, so pre-washing is essential. Overlock or zig-zag stitch across the cut ends of the fabric to reduce fraying when pre-washing. When pressing linen, spritz the fabric with water and use a steam iron. Over-pressing can give the fabric a slick, shiny appearance. To avoid this, use a pressing cloth.

❊ VELVET AND VELVETEEN

Soft and lustrous, velvet and velveteen are wonderful fabrics that can work well in certain quilting projects.

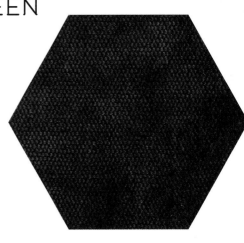

CHARACTERISTICS

These soft fabrics are woven in a double format and then cut apart into two pieces of cloth, each with a napped pile of threads. Take note of the fabric's nap. If the nap faces different directions, it can change the look and feel of your finished project.

TYPES

VELVET – most commonly made from silk, this textile is expensive and luxurious. Available in many colours, it is traditionally used in crazy quilts with embroidery embellishment. Because it requires dry cleaning and special handling, it does not lend itself to many patchwork applications.

VELVETEEN – woven from cotton, velveteen is soft and has more 'give' than velvet. It is also more affordable and easy to find. Manufactured in a wide range of solid colours and an increasing number of vibrant prints, velveteen is machine washable, making it a great textile to use in all sorts of quilts.

SEWING TIPS

When working with velvet and velveteen, use a fine, sharp needle and reduce the pressure on the presser foot so as not to smash the delicate pile. Sew in the direction of the nap, not against it. A walking foot is helpful to ensure the fabric feeds evenly through the machine.

CARE TIPS

Take care when pressing velvet and velveteen, as heat can destroy the pile. Place the fabrics face down on a towel and press from the wrong side.

 # DENIM

Denim is not only for jeans. This sturdy, cotton fabric comes in various weights and colours and can be used with most quilting patterns. Buy new yardage off the bolt or cut up and repurpose denim jeans, skirts and shirts for use in patchwork quilts.

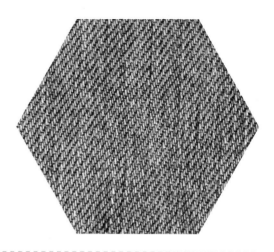

CHARACTERISTICS

Characterised by its dark blue colour, denim has a dense, twill weave with a diagonal rib. Because the dark warp threads are woven with white weft threads, it appears blue on its right side and white on its wrong side.

PROS

Denim will stand up to heavy use and is a great choice when making quilts that will get a lot of wear. It is available in many different weights, and various shades of blue and other colours.

CONS

Heavyweight fabrics like denim produce bulky seams and are not suitable for hand piecing and quilting.

SEWING TIPS

When sewing denim, use a denim needle for your machine and increase the stitch length. Using a walking foot for piecing will keep the fabric from shifting. Because denim frays easily, it is important to increase the seam allowance to 13 mm (½ in). Press all seams open to reduce the bulk. Machine quilt or tie your project.

CARE TIPS

Wash new denim at least twice to reduce dye bleeding and soften the hand of the fabric.

 # CORDUROY

Narrow and pinwale corduroys are the best choices for quilting because they closely resemble quilting cottons in weight.

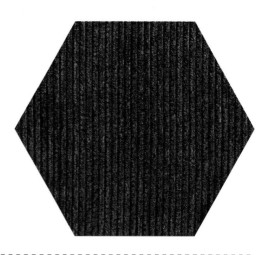

CHARACTERISTICS

Available in various weights, corduroy has a ribbed texture. The ridges, or wales, are made from a cut fibre, similar to velvet, which has a nap. Wales can vary in thickness from thick to thin, and the fabric is classified by the number of wales per centimetre.

PROS

Corduroy is cosy, soft to the touch, and adds a nice tactile quality to quilts. It can be purchased in solid colours and some prints and is an extremely durable fabric.

CONS

Because it has a nap, working with corduroy can be a challenge. When looking at corduroy from different directions, the colour may appear different. Heavier, wider-wale corduroys will produce bulky seams, especially if multiple points meet in one place.

SEWING TIPS

Corduroy can creep when it is sewn, leaving you with inaccurate and crooked seams. Use many pins and a walking foot when piecing to help battle creeping. To help prevent fraying, increase the seam allowance to 13 mm (½ in).

CARE TIPS

Corduroys are known to shrink considerably, so pre-wash the fabric. When pressing, use steam and a towel as a pressing cloth to preserve the fabric's nap.

# SILK

There are many different types of silk that are suitable for quilting and are readily available to purchase by the metre. Additionally, second-hand silk blouses, men's ties and women's scarves can be cut up and reused in different patchwork applications.

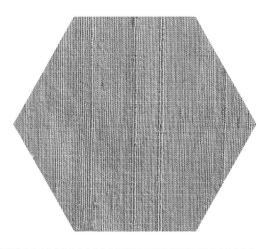

CHARACTERISTICS

Silk comes in many different types and weights. With its subtle sheen, soft hand and beautiful drape, silk is a luxurious textile to use in quilts.

TYPES OF SILK

Dupioni silk is woven from two different-coloured threads and comes in bright, rich colours with a beautiful, iridescent sheen. Intentional slubs give this silk a subtle texture.

China or Habotai silk is available in several weights, and is the classic silk seen in kimonos and other apparel. It is beautifully soft, drapes well and has a smooth, lustrous finish.

Raw silk or silk noil is heavier and stiffer than other silks. It has a slightly nubby texture. Its off-white colour stands up beautifully to painting and dyeing.

PROS

Silk is warm and soft to the touch. It is luxurious, but still durable enough to stand up to frequent use. Available in deep, rich colours, woven silks have a slight sheen and most substrates stand up to dyeing and painting well.

CONS

Working with silk can be a bit tricky, as it is slippery and frays easily.

SUITABLE APPLICATIONS

Silk can be used in just about any pattern and piecing method.

SEWING TIPS

When sewing silk, use a Microtex or sharp needle with a slim, sharp point. Stabilise your pieces with a lightweight interfacing to prevent stretching and use a larger seam allowance to help prevent fraying. Use several pins and a walking foot to keep the fabric from slipping and shifting while you sew.

CARE TIPS

Pre-wash your silk fabrics in the same manner that you will launder your quilt in the future to avoid shrinking and dye bleeding. When ironing silk, press it at a low heat without steam to prevent water spots and scorching.

 # WOOL

Wool is a good fabric choice for quilts. Woven into fabrics that range in weight, it is available in myriad colours. Additionally, felted sweaters and wool clothing can be repurposed into fabric for the modern quilter to use in their designs.

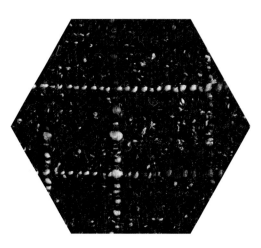

CHARACTERISTICS

Wool is a natural fibre that comes from sheep and other animals such as goats, alpacas, rabbits and camels. Warm, comfortable and soft to the touch, it has been used in quilts for many years.

PROS

Wool fabric is extremely warm and a good insulator. It stretches easily, but will retain its shape. Wool also absorbs moisture and is naturally fire and dirt resistant, making it very durable. Because wool accepts dye easily, it is available in many deep and rich colours. Felted wools will not fray and can be machine washed.

CONS

Heavy wools can produce bulky patchwork seams. If you are using wool that is not felted, it will require special laundering techniques or dry cleaning.

SUITABLE APPLICATIONS

Wool fabrics can be used for just about any kind of quilting, and they work well in patchwork designs. Felted wools are a wonderful choice for appliqué and decorative embellishments.

SEWING TIPS

Sewing with wool is very straightforward. If you are using lightweight wool, it can be treated like similar-weight woven fabrics. Heavier wools will produce bulky seams, so abutting the pieces and sewing them with a flat seam and zig-zag stitch may give you a better result. On loosely woven wools, such as tweeds, use a larger seam allowance to keep the fabric from fraying.

CARE TIPS

Wool fabrics must be pretreated before sewing in the same manner you plan to launder the quilt in the future. Steam and excess heat will shrink unfelted wool. To avoid this, wash wool in cold water and hang it to dry. Dry cleaning is also acceptable. When pressing wool, use a low heat setting and a pressing cloth.

# HAND-DYED FABRICS

Many natural fibres take dyes well and, as a result, more and more fabrics are being hand dyed for quilting. While hand-dyed silks, wools and linens are commercially available, the most commonly used hand-dyed fabric in quilting is cotton.

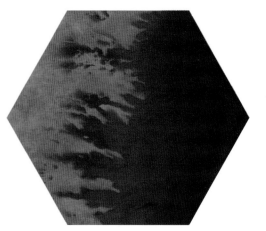

CHARACTERISTICS
Hand-dyed fabrics are vibrant, with rich colours and, often, interesting designs. Batiks are dyed using a wax resist to create pattern and the cottons used for them are tightly woven with a light, silky feel.

PROS
One-of-a-kind hand-dyed fabrics are exactly that: unique! They can be used like other quilting cottons and work well with hand and machine piecing and quilting techniques.

CONS
Due to the nature of hand dyeing, colour variations may occur throughout a length of fabric. Darker colours such as blues and reds may bleed when laundered. Also, hand-dyed batiks are often more expensive than standard quilting cottons.

SEWING TIPS
Because batiks are tightly woven, it is advisable to use a smaller needle when hand quilting or a Microtex needle when machine sewing.

CARE TIPS
Pre-wash hand-dyed fabrics with a dye magnet or a commercial colour fixative to reduce the risk of dye bleeding.

Top: Mandala quilt. **Bottom:** Colorplay quilt. Both by Anne Lullie, made with hand-dyed cotton and silk fabrics.

2: YARDAGE AND MEASURING

How much fabric do I need? That is the dilemma many quilters face at the cutting table. Not to worry – this chapter is packed full of guidelines and formulas that will help you determine just how many metres of fabric it will take to make your quilt. From how many shapes per metre to how much wadding you need, and everything in between: it's all covered.

CALCULATING QUILT SIZES

When designing your quilt, it is important to keep in mind where it will be used. Bed quilts in particular take some planning to ensure that they cover the mattress in the manner you desire. Other quilts, such as throws and wall hangings, can be made to whatever size you see fit.

To make bedding universal, mattresses are made to industry-standard widths and lengths, but different styles of bed quilts will require some adjustments. Coverlets fall about 7.5 cm (3 in) below the bottom of the mattress, whereas bedspreads have a longer drop, often falling to 13 mm (½ in) from the floor. Quilts that include a pillow tuck need an additional 25–45 cm (10–18 in) of length to accommodate the pillow and the tuck. Platform beds may need a quilt with extra length for tucking under the mattress, and day bed quilts may have a drop on only one side.

Throw quilts vary in size, ranging from 102 × 152 cm (40 × 60 in) up to single bed size or bigger. It is a good idea to think about who will use the finished quilt, and how. Want a throw for napping on the sofa? It probably needs to be long enough for an adult to lie under. Beach quilts and other such throws might be square and large enough for a family to sit on.

A final thing to consider is shrinkage. Cotton fabrics and wadding will shrink up to 5 per cent with laundering. Keep this in mind when planning the size of your quilt so it won't be too small after it is first washed.

TAKING MEASUREMENTS

Mattress width and length measurements are universal (see the chart on page 33), but there is a great variation in mattress depths. Standard and older mattresses are typically between 20 cm (8 in) and 30 cm (12 in) high, whereas newer, pillow-top versions may be as deep as 45 cm (18 in). You'll need to measure your mattress depth to ensure a well-fitting bed quilt. For throw-sized quilts, measure a favourite blanket for size or pull out a tape measure to see what looks right.

CALCULATING BED QUILT MEASUREMENTS

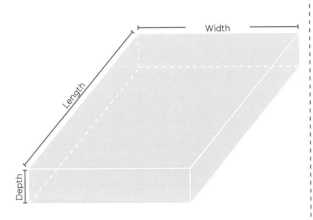

1. Begin with the mattress's width and length.

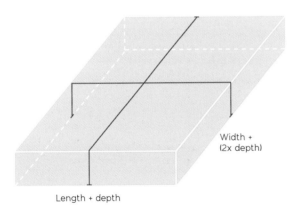

2. Add the depth of the mattress twice to the width (once for the left side, once for the right side) and once to the length (for the bottom).

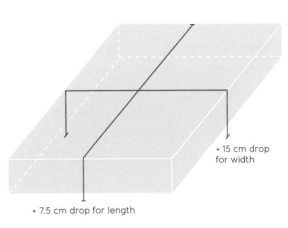

+ 15 cm drop for width

+ 7.5 cm drop for length

3. Add the drop (7.5 cm/3 in or more depending on the style of quilt) twice to the width (once for the left side, once for the right side) and once to the length (for the bottom).

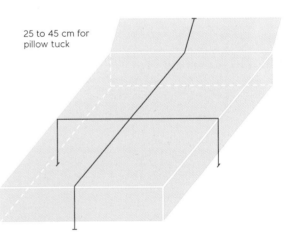

25 to 45 cm for pillow tuck

4. If you want a pillow tuck, add it once to the length.

5. Subtotal the width and length measurements and multiply each by 1.05 to add 5 per cent for shrinkage. Round up to the nearest full unit of measurement.

USING STANDARD MATTRESS AND QUILT SIZES

What if you are making a quilt as a gift or you aren't able to measure the mattress for a custom fit? Don't fret – by using standard mattress sizes and typical quilt measurements, you can confidently sew a quilt that should fit just about any bed.

Mattress sizes (UK)	Width × length	Quilt size
Cot	74 × 132 cm (29 × 52 in)	91 × 137 cm (36 × 54 in)
Single	90 × 190 cm (35 × 75 in)	165 × 224 cm (65 × 88 in)
Small double	120 × 190 cm (47 × 75 in)	165 × 224 cm (65 × 88 in)
Double	135 × 190 cm (53 × 75 in)	203 × 224 cm (80 × 88 in)
King	150 × 200 cm (59 × 79 in)	218 × 236 cm (86 × 93 in)
Super king	180 × 200 cm (71 × 79 in)	236 × 264 cm (93 × 104 in)

CALCULATING BLOCKS PER QUILT

Once you have determined how big the quilt should be, it's time to break your quilt down into smaller pieces. Generally, most quilt patterns have blocks that measure a particular size. By taking the finished quilt measurements and dividing them by that block size, you will know how many blocks you need for your quilt.

Of course, not all measurements can be divided evenly. If the resulting quilt will only be a centimetre or two shorter or bigger in any direction, it will still fit well. Go ahead and make it without any adjustments. If the quilt is substantially smaller, you can enlarge it by adding sashing between the blocks or borders around the quilt's perimeter. If you are unsure of what to do, grab some graph paper and pencils and sketch your options. You can also start making blocks and lay them out to see what looks best to you. You might even use masking tape on the floor to give you an idea of the finished size of a quilt. Often a visual reference is easier to understand than a list of measurements.

25 cm

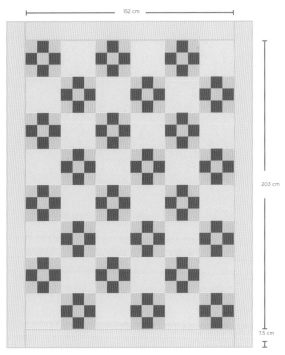

152 cm

203 cm

7.5 cm

For a single bed quilt, add 7.5 to 10 cm borders to each side of the 165 x 224 cm quilt top

 # CALCULATING SHAPES PER METRE

When trying to figure out how much fabric your quilt requires, it is good to know a few basic things. Knowing the width of the fabric you are using is essential when calculating how much yardage your pieces will require.

As a rule, most quilter's cottons come in a standard width in the range of 100–110 cm (40–44 in). Other fabric substrates, such as voile and linen, are more likely to come in widths of 137–152 cm (54–60 in). It's best to check your fabric's width before you start calculating and cutting.

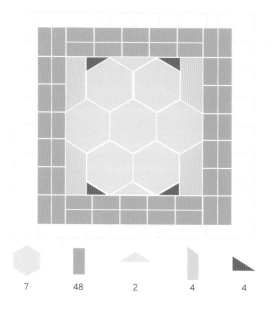

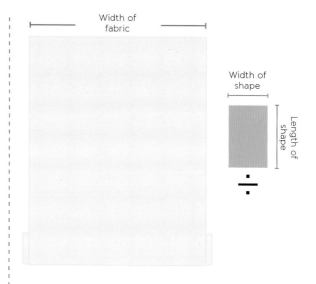

COUNT UP YOUR SHAPES

It's important to know how many of each shape you will need for your quilt. Sketch your design digitally or on graph paper for a quick visual reference. It may be helpful to use different colours to indicate different printed and solid fabrics. Make notations of each shape's size, specifically the width and height, and tally the total number required for each piece and each fabric at the bottom or side of your sketch. Do not forget to include the seam allowances.

CALCULATING YARDAGE

1. First, figure out how many shapes fit across the width of your fabric. To do this, take the width of your fabric and divide it by the width of your shape. For example, if your fabric is 107 cm (42 in) wide and you are cutting a rectangle that is 13 cm (5 in) wide, you can fit eight rectangles across one width of fabric (107/13 or 42/5 = 8.25).

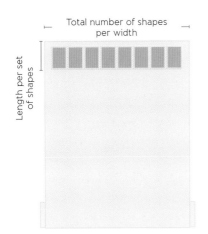

Total number of shapes per width

Length per set of shapes

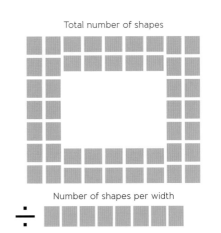

Total number of shapes

Number of shapes per width

2. Next, using the shape's length, you can determine how long each strip of fabric will be. If the length of the rectangle is 18 cm (7 in), you will be able to get eight rectangles per 18 cm (7 in) length of fabric.

4. Finally, multiply the number of strips required (six) by each strip's length (18 cm /7 in) to get the total length of fabric (6 × 18 cm = 108 cm or 6 × 7 in = 42 in). Divide by 100 cm (108/100 cm = 1.08 m) or 36 in (42/36 in = 1.1 yd) for the yardage. To account for shrinkage and trueing up the fabric, it is a good idea to round this up to the nearest quarter or half metre (eg 1.1 m is rounded to 1.5 m).

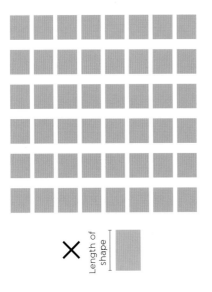

Length of shape

3. To calculate the total yardage you need, divide the total number of shapes by the number of shapes per strip. If you need 48 rectangles, divide that by eight (48/8 = 6).

YARDAGE FOR OTHER SHAPES

For half-square triangles, multiply the number of squares per strip by two. Likewise, one cut square will yield four quarter-square triangles. To calculate the number of other polygons per metre, measure the shape's maximum width and length and plug those numbers into the formula. For circles, use the diameter for both measurements. You can also stack and stagger shapes such as diamonds, hexagons and other non-square-based triangles to minimise waste. Cut a few templates from paper and lay them out on the fabric or make a sketch to scale to see how many shapes you can get from each strip. Directional prints and fussy cutting will require more fabric.

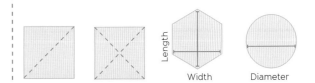

Length

Width

Diameter

USING PRE-CUTS

Pre-cut fabric is a wonderful time-saver when making quilts. Often sold in bundles, the fabrics usually represent an entire fabric line, which gives quilters the opportunity to use many different prints without having to buy yardage of each one. Pre-cut bundles also make matching colours a breeze, as they are often colour-coordinated.

Because the pieces are cut to size, pre-cuts can save you time cutting and there is less fabric waste. The units can be sewn together as they are or, with larger pre-cuts, further divided into smaller pieces. To determine how many shapes a particular pre-cut will yield, use the formula outlined on pages 34–35.

Larger pre-cuts that will be cut into multiple shapes can be pre-washed to reduce shrinkage and dye discharge. Washing smaller pre-cuts is a bit trickier. Hand washing, while slightly tedious, is the best option. Handle the fabric gently to avoid frayed ends, and air dry to reduce shrinkage and tangling. Press all pre-cuts before using them and take time to square fat quarters and fat eighths to ensure they are on-grain.

COMMON PRE-CUTS

Fat quarters: Approximately 56 x 50 cm (22 x 18 in), fat quarters yield more usable fabric for quilting than a straight quarter metre would (112 x 25 cm/ 44 x 9 in). They can be found for sale in bunches or individually. Many quilting stores will even cut fat quarters off the bolt if you ask. Fat quarters are a great way to incorporate small amounts of multiple prints into one project, often with fabric to spare.

Fat eighths: Half of a fat quarter, these ⅛-metre pieces measure 56 × 25 cm (22 × 9 in). Not as readily available as fat quarters, they are most often sold in bundles. Fat eighths work well for subdividing into smaller shapes.

Charm squares: These 12.5 cm (5 in) squares of fabric are often sewn as is or cut into half-square triangles. They are commercially available in small stacks and are sometimes traded between quilters.

Layer cakes: Sold in bundles, layer cakes are 25 cm (10 in) squares of fabric. They are often used in their entirety or cut into smaller squares and rectangles.

Jelly roll strips: Measuring 6.4 × 112 cm (2½ × 44 in), or the width of the fabric, these long, skinny pre-cuts work well for strip piecing and Log Cabin quilt blocks. They can also be cut into smaller squares and rectangles for a multitude of different uses.

CALCULATING SASHING AND BORDERS

Calculating the yardage required for sashing and borders is done in a similar manner as calculating shapes per metre. You need to know how wide the border and sashing fabric is, and how many sashing strips or borders you need. Additionally, it is important to consider whether the sashing and borders will be oriented with the grain or against it. This will determine how the fabric is cut and, consequently, the yardage requirement may vary.

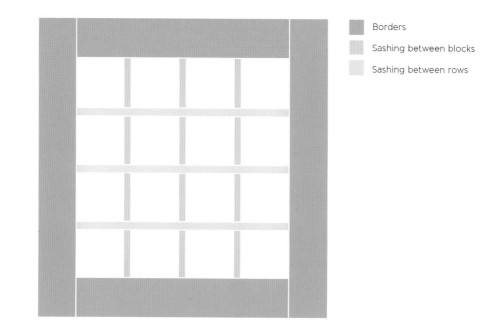

■ Borders

▨ Sashing between blocks

▨ Sashing between rows

SASHING

1. Sketch out your quilt by hand or digitally. Count how many sashing strips are between the blocks in each row and make a note of their width and length, including any seam allowances. For the purpose of calculating sashing, the width of the strip is the measurement that runs with the fabric's crosswise grain.

2. Next, count the sashing strips between rows, noting their width and length measurements. If they are the same size as the sashing strips between blocks, add the two numbers together and calculate the yardage required by following the formula for calculating shapes per metre on pages 34–35.

3. If the sashing strips between rows are different dimensions from the sashing strips between blocks, calculate each amount separately. When using plain sashing between rows, you may have to sew two or more fabric strips together to make the strip long enough. If this is the case, do not forget to add in the seam allowances that this piecing requires.

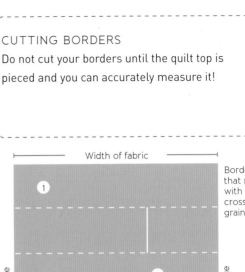

Borders that run with the lengthways grain

Width of fabric

Selvedge edge

Selvedge edge

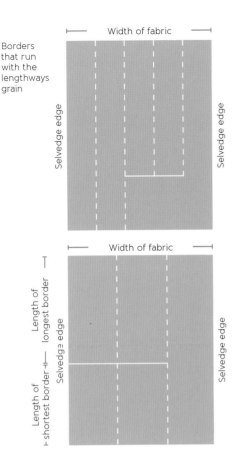

Width of fabric

Length of longest border

Length of shortest border

Selvedge edge

Selvedge edge

CUTTING BORDERS

Do not cut your borders until the quilt top is pieced and you can accurately measure it!

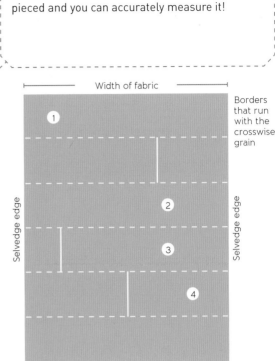

Width of fabric

Borders that run with the crosswise grain

Selvedge edge

Selvedge edge

BORDERS

1. Refer to the sketch of the quilt for the width and length of the borders.

2. If the borders will run with the lengthways grain of the fabric, the yardage is easy to calculate. Divide the fabric's width by the width of the border to see how many borders will fit across the fabric.

3. If this number is four or more, take the length measurement of the longest border and divide it by 100 to convert it into metres. The resulting number is the yardage required for the borders.

4. If this number is less than four, take the length of the shorter borders and add it to the length of the longer borders. Divide the sum by 100 to determine how many metres are required.

5. When you're using the fabric's crosswise grain for borders, take the border's length measurement and divide it by the fabric's width to calculate how many widths of fabric you need for one border. Don't forget to add on the seam allowance if the border needs to be pieced.

6. Take the number of fabric widths and multiply it by the border's width measurement to determine how many metres are required for the one border. Double this yardage to account for the corresponding border on the opposite side of the quilt.

7. Repeat these steps to find the yardage required for the other pair of borders. Add both amounts together for the total yardage requirement. Always round up to the next half metre to allow for squaring and shrinkage.

❖ CALCULATING WADDING, BACKING FABRIC AND BINDING

Once you have determined how much fabric your quilt top will require, it is time to think about the other components of the quilt. You will need to purchase wadding and fabric for the quilt back as well as fabric for the binding. With a few quick calculations you will know exactly how much you need to finish your quilt.

WADDING

Wadding sold from the bolt is available in different widths. The most common is 229 cm (90 in) wide; however, it can also be found in smaller and larger widths. To calculate the yardage to buy, you need to know the width of the wadding and the measurements of your quilt top. Add at least 15 cm (6 in) to both the width and the length to ensure that the wadding is larger than the quilt top on all sides.

If one or both measurements are smaller than the width of the wadding, take the larger measurement and divide it by 100. The resulting number will be the yardage of wadding you require. If both measurements are larger than the wadding's width, you will need to piece the wadding so it is large enough for your project.

Bed size	Standard wadding size
Cot	114 × 152 cm (45 × 60 in)
Single	183 × 229 cm (72 × 90 in)
Double	206 × 244 cm (81 × 96 in)
King	229 × 274 cm (90 × 108 in)
Super king	305 × 305 cm (120 × 120 in)

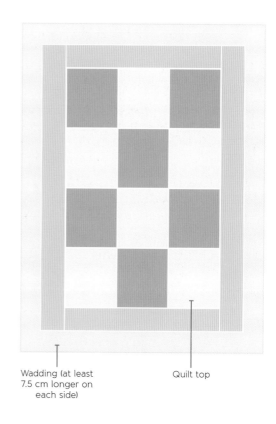

Wadding (at least 7.5 cm longer on each side)

Quilt top

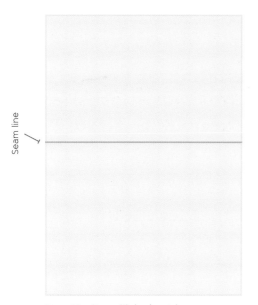

Seam line

Pieced backing with horizontal seam

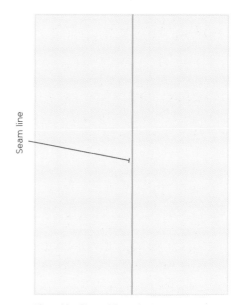

Seam line

Pieced backing with vertical seam

BACKING FABRIC

Like wadding, backing fabric should be a few centimetres larger than the quilt top on all sides. Add 15 cm (6 in) to the quilt top's width and length measurements to determine the size of the backing.

Most quilt backs require piecing, as standard quilting cottons measure 107 cm (42 in) wide. If you are lucky enough to find a wider fabric that won't require any piecing, then calculating how many metres to buy is simple. Decide which way the quilt will best fit the backing fabric, and then measure how long the fabric needs to be. Divide this measurement by 100 to calculate how many metres you need.

Pieced quilt backs have either horizontal or vertical seams. Draw a sketch to see which option will work better for your project. For vertical seams, take the finished backing width measurement and divide it by the width of the fabric. This will tell you how many widths you need. The length of each width should be equal to the length of the finished backing. Multiply the total number of widths by the length measurement and divide it by 100 to get the total metres needed.

With horizontal seams, fabric is often turned sideways so that the width between selvedges is used for the length. The calculation is the same as for vertical seams except that you treat the backing's width measurement as its length, and vice versa.

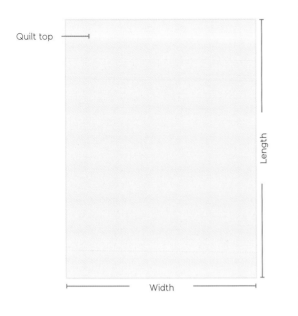

Quilt top

Length

Width

Selvedge

Selvedge

Width of fabric

BINDING

To calculate the amount of fabric you need for binding, you'll need to find out the perimeter of your quilt. Measure the width and the length, and then add them as follows: (2 × w) + (2 × l) + 30 cm (12 in) = total length of binding required

For cross-grain binding: Divide the total binding length by the width of the binding fabric to determine how many strips you need, rounding up to the next whole number. Multiply the number of fabric strips by their width to see the total length of fabric. Divide that number by 100 to determine how many metres to buy.

Selvedge

Selvedge

Width of fabric

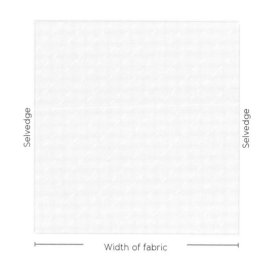

Selvedge

Selvedge

Width of fabric

For straight-grain binding: Divide the width of the binding fabric by the width of the binding strip, to determine how many strips per width of fabric. If the result is a fraction, round down to the previous whole number. Now divide the total binding length by the number of strips for the total fabric length required. Add 12.5 cm to this to account for piecing strips and then divide by 100 to transform cm to metres.

For bias binding: Multiply the total length of binding by the width of the binding strips. Take the square root of the resulting number and add 5 cm to it. Then round up to the next whole number. For continuous bias binding, cut a square to this measurement. For pieced bias binding, buy fabric to this length. Divide by 100 to convert it from cm to metres.

✿ 3: CARING FOR FABRICS

Have you ever pulled a quilt out of the laundry to find that a fabric has bled or that it has shrunk in an uneven way? A ruined quilt has to be the biggest heartbreak a quilter can suffer after spending hours and hours sewing a project. Although nothing is guaranteed, knowing how to care for your fabric should help prevent you from being brokenhearted.

❈ PRE-WASHING FABRIC

Quilters are divided when it comes to deciding whether cotton quilting fabrics should be pre-washed or not. There is no right answer. It is truly a matter of personal preference, but there are some pros and cons to consider before choosing which method is right for you.

PROS

Cotton fabrics will shrink, and often at different rates. Pre-washing the fabric helps avoid uneven shrinkage, which may cause puckering and distortion when a quilt is first laundered. The resulting quilt will have a smoother, flatter finish.

Some colours, such as reds, blues and purples, may bleed when first washed. By pre-washing the fabric, you may be able to remove some excess dyes, but it is not always a guarantee of colourfastness. When in doubt, perform a bleed test to ensure that your fabric is colourfast (see page 46).

Pre-washing also removes sizing and other chemical protectors from your fabric. Not only is this helpful for quilters who are sensitive to chemicals, it also makes the fabric easier to handle for hand piecing and hand quilting.

CONS

If you prefer your quilt to have a vintage, crinkly look, this will be less noticeable with pre-washed fabrics.

Fabric straight off the bolt is easier to cut and sew. Its crisp hand makes machine sewing simple as well.

Pre-washing is not a guarantee of colourfastness. Some fabrics will still bleed no matter whether they are pre-washed or not.

When using small pre-cuts such as charm squares and jelly roll strips, pre-washing tends to fray and tangle the fabrics, making them less usable.

Why bother pre-washing fabric for a quilting project that will never be laundered? This is something to consider when making art quilts and wall hangings that you don't plan on washing.

HOW TO PRE-WASH FABRIC

Separate dark and light-coloured fabrics. Wash them in cool water with a mild detergent. Tumble dry on low heat, fold neatly to store and then press before using. If you plan on using the fabric right away, removing it from the dryer when it is still damp and pressing it immediately will reduce the amount of wrinkles. Line drying is perfectly acceptable as well.

OTHER TEXTILES

If your quilt is constructed with fabrics that contain fibres other than cotton, it is important that you care for them as indicated on the bolt. Remember that natural fibres such as linen and wool are more prone to shrinkage than synthetics. Silks, velvets and other speciality fabrics may need to be dry cleaned. When in doubt, pre-wash the fabrics in the manner in which you plan to launder the finished quilt.

✿ TESTING FOR COLOURFASTNESS

Saturated, vividly coloured cotton fabric may bleed when wet. It is important to test for colourfastness before using these fabrics in your quilt, as you do not want them bleeding onto other fabrics when the quilt is laundered.

To perform a bleed test, prepare a bowl of warm soapy water using the same mild detergent that you would use to launder the finished project. Submerge a small piece of the fabric in the water and let it sit for 30 minutes. Remove the fabric from the water and check to see if the water is discoloured. If it is, then you know that the fabric bleeds. If the water is not discoloured, place the fabric onkitchen paper to dry. If the colour migrates from the fabric to the paper, the fabric is not colourfast. If both the water and the paper remain free from dyes, you have a colourfast fabric that you can use in your quilt without worrying about bleeding.

PREVENTING DYE BLEEDING

If the fabric you want to use fails the bleed test, you have a couple of options available to you. The first is to not use the fabric in your quilt. While this may not be ideal, it is certainly the safest option to make sure that it will not continue to transfer colour to other fabrics.

You can also pre-wash the fabric repeatedly using a dye magnet or colour catcher. Dye magnets, made from white, untreated cotton fabric, will attract all the excess dye in the water and trap it. If you choose this route, bleed test the fabric after each wash to see whether any excess dye remains. It may take many wash cycles before your fabric is colourfast. Do remember that excessive washing can weaken the fibres and dull the colour, too.

Using a commercial dye fixative on your fabrics when you initially wash them will prevent colour bleeding during washing. However, this is a pre-treating option and cannot be used once the quilt has been pieced.

If bleeding occurs once a quilt has been finished and laundered, it can be difficult to remove. Specialist detergents keep excess dye particles in suspension, not allowing them to adhere to fabrics, and may help rectify colour bleeding in quilts. Other water additives such as vinegar and salt can sometimes keep bleeding at bay, but are often temporary solutions.

CARING FOR YOUR FABRIC

After purchasing fabric for a particular project or as an addition to your growing fabric stash, it will need to be stored until you are ready to use it. By following a few simple storage guidelines, you can keep your fabric in excellent condition.

Sunlight is the biggest environmental factor to consider when deciding how and where to store your fabric. Any fabric that is exposed to light is in danger of fading. Keeping your fabrics in a dark room, a wardrobe or a closed cabinet will keep fading to a minimum. If open shelving is your best storage option, occasionally refold your fabrics to eliminate crease marks and discourage fading.

Another factor to consider is the environment in which the fabric will be stored. Make sure that your fabric is away from insects and other pests that may harm your stash.

Cool, dry air is desirable to keep fabrics looking their best. Cold, damp basements and hot, humid attics are uncontrolled climates and should be avoided when possible. It is important that the fabric is able to breathe. While lidded plastic bins and cardboard boxes are convenient and stackable, if they are left closed for an extended period of time, the fabrics may take on strange smells, change colour or disintegrate.

STORAGE

How you organise your fabric is a matter of personal preference, but there are some things to consider. Some quilters like to separate their fabrics by colour, and others prefer to do it by size or even type of fabric. You could sort smaller pieces of prints by colour, with a different section for solids. Then larger pieces can be stored on different shelves so it is easy to see which fabrics might work for quilt backs and binding. Felts and wools can have their own spot, as can other speciality fabrics. Develop a system and put it in place so you know what you have and exactly where it is when you need it.

MALKA DUBRAWSKY

Malka Dubrawsky is a Texas-based fibre artist, fabric designer and author. In addition to her sewing business, she creates her own surface designs and hand dyes and prints fabrics in her home studio.

Malka began sewing after graduating with a degree in printmaking. Without the facilities to continue making prints, she turned to fabric, needle and thread to convert her drawings into textiles. She taught herself to sew first and, after a while, to quilt.

Not satisfied with the fabrics available, Malka decided to create her own surface designs by dyeing and overdyeing fabrics. Using wax and other resists, she produces unique fabric in original colours and patterns to use in her quilts. Her use of different dyeing techniques gives her work incredible depth.

Malka does not like to limit herself by choosing a particular colour palette. She may sometimes focus on contrasting colours or combine warm and cool colours, but that is the extent of her rules. She likes to experiment with value and how it can make a quilt block pop out or recede into the background. Mostly, though, she just follows her instincts about which colours 'seem to sing when they're placed alongside each other'. She also plays with prints and solids. Her knack for combining colour and pattern gives her designs their signature look.

Malka's quilts are fresh interpretations of conventional blocks and shapes. The way she approaches her designs stems from her desire to put a modern twist on traditionally rooted quilting patterns. She loves to play around with possibilities and many of her patterns gain a modern edge from improvisational piecing. By putting her measuring tools to the side and cutting freehand, Malka achieves stunning and unique results. She also likes to change the scale of commonly designed patchwork blocks. By enlarging simple motifs, such as a Shoo Fly or Log Cabin block, to a super size, Malka remakes older block styles into something entirely of the moment.

'I think all my design decisions are outgrowths of a single question: what if? What if I took a traditional block and blew it up out of all proportion? What if I put aside my measuring tools and just freehand cut my fabric? What if I used value to make certain parts of a block or design disappear into the background? For me, it's about answering that simple question.'

Clockwise from top left: Scrap Box; Pinwheel; Pieces of 8.

RITA HODGE

Quilter Rita Hodge (based in Melbourne, Australia) journals her quilting process on the blog Red Pepper Quilts. Begun in 2009, the blog features Rita's works-in-progress and finished quilts, which she sells in her Etsy shop. Her quilts are traditionally inspired with simple shapes, bright colours and gorgeous fabrics.

Rita grew up in the Netherlands with her three sisters. An accomplished seamstress, her mother not only made her daughters' clothing, but also spent her evenings cross-stitching and knitting. Although surrounded by her mother's making, Rita did not begin sewing until she was in her early thirties. When her children began primary school, she volunteered to make a block for the school's annual raffle quilt. As the years went on, Rita became more involved with this project and started a sewing group with fellow parents.

Her first quilt was based on a pattern from a magazine and included appliqué with blanket stitch and hand quilting. Not only was it her first quilt, it was also her last one with hand quilting. Rita likes to work at her own pace, trying new techniques and figuring out what she does and doesn't like to make as she goes. She particularly enjoys simple, repetitive patchwork piecing and using scraps. All her quilts are pieced and quilted on her domestic sewing machine.

Rita's quilt designs feature basic shapes inspired by traditional quilts. While her quilts are contemporary, they do not have a modern minimalist look. Instead, they are a wonderful combination of prints and shapes that puts the focus on the fabrics Rita uses instead of the quilt's pattern. Rita quilts most of her projects with straight lines that outline the blocks' seams, or a simple crosshatch pattern.

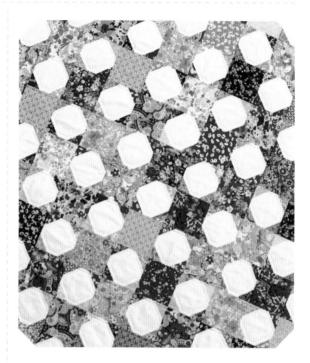

For inspiration, Rita looks to her fabric collection. She views it as much more than a group of fabrics. Instead, she sees it as a catalogue of colours and designs that she can pull from to create interesting quilts. She has a knack for pairing fabrics and will stack various combinations of prints to jump-start her creativity. She says, 'I enjoy editing these fabric stacks and, although not all turn into quilts, I think some of my better work has come from a compilation of fabric that has evolved over a week or so of sitting on my cutting table.'

Opposite: Bloomsbury Gardens. **Clockwise from top left:** Labyrinth; Fundraiser quilt; Rainbow Ripple.

2

SECTION TWO
COLOURS

4: COLOUR THEORY

A little knowledge about colours and how they work together can be instrumental in developing a colour palette to use in any project, quilts included. Everyone, even those with a natural ability to combine colours, can benefit from ideas about how colour works and where to find inspiration for cohesive colour palettes.

COLOUR WHEEL

To choose the colours you will use in a quilt, it is often best to start at the beginning: the colour wheel. With a basic knowledge of how colours work together, you can confidently choose a colour palette for your project.

MIXING COLOURS

The colour wheel is an organised visual tool to help us make sense of colour. Each of its twelve parts represents a colour. The three primary colours are the building blocks that all other colours come from. When two primary colours are mixed together, the result is a secondary colour. The final colours on the wheel are a mix of primary and secondary and are called tertiary colours.

DIFFERENT COLOUR SCHEMES

The warm colours run from red-violet to yellow on the colour wheel. These colours tend to stand out and look more dominant when used in a quilt. The other half of the colour wheel makes up the cool colours. These blues and greens tend to recede more.

Complementary colours are located across from one another on the wheel. These colour pairs are visually pleasing and have high contrast between them. Together they create a vibrant look, but they can be hard to balance in large doses at full saturation.

A monochromatic colour scheme contains variations in lightness and saturation of a single colour. The colours are balanced and look good together, but the lack of contrast can make it boring. Use many shades of these in your quilt for visual interest.

Analogous colours are side by side on the wheel. These combinations are often found in nature and are harmonious to the eye. They are richer than monochromatic schemes, but often lack contrast. Let one colour be dominant and use others as accents.

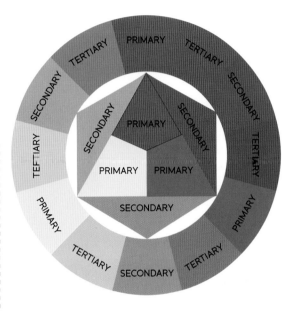

TINTS, SHADES, TONES

Only true colours are represented on the wheel, but there are many others to consider. Lighter, darker, brighter – all are characteristics to consider when choosing colours for a quilt. When you add white to a colour to make it lighter it is called a tint. A shade is the result of adding black to a colour to make it darker and a tone is what you get when you add grey.

CONTEXT

One other thing to consider when using the colour wheel to develop a colour palette is context. Maybe a colour is brighter against black and duller against white, or appears to have more red in it when it is against a warm colour. It's a good idea to try colours against one another to see how they change.

CHOOSING COLOUR PALETTES

The colour wheel and a knowledge of basic colour theory are great tools to use when choosing a colour palette for your quilt, but there are other ways of picking a colour scheme, too. By taking a look at what visually inspires and excites you, it is easy to determine appealing colour combinations.

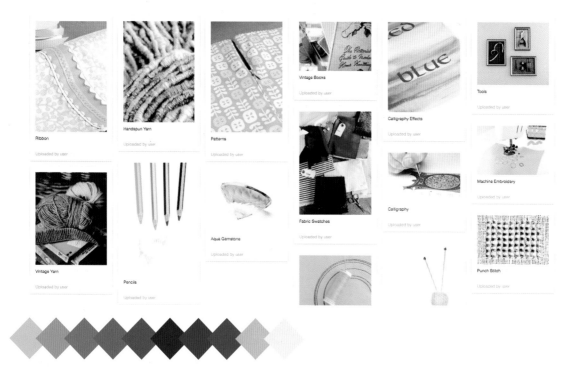

COLLECT INSPIRATION

One good exercise to help you develop a colour palette is to create an inspiration board. Gather items and photographs that inspire you. These could be pages from a magazine, bits of ephemera, paint chips, items found in nature or small curios from around your home. Group these items together and take a closer look. If you can, pin them to a bulletin board or tape them to your wall. You could also arrange them on a table. Consider using a digital camera to take a photo of your grouping. There are several online tools, such as Pinterest, Polyvore or Mosaic Maker, which allow you to create digital 'mood boards', and these are all great ways to catalogue your inspirations. Once you are happy with your arrangement, take a step back and see if a theme emerges. Do you notice any similarities and patterns? Are the items different shades of one colour, like lots of different tones of blue, or are there multiple colours with more contrast? Pick out the dominant one or two colours and start building your quilt's colour palette around those. Add accents and contrast with other colours from your inspiration board.

TAKE PHOTOS

Another way to create a colour palette for a quilt is to use a photograph as a starting point. Photographs of nature can help you replicate the colours of a particular season or flower in a quilt, just as a photo of toy cars or bright marbles might be wonderful inspiration for a child's quilt. Choose a photo that speaks to you, and in it you will find colour combinations that are pleasing to you. Use some coloured pencils or markers to draw swatches of the different colours from your photo on white paper until you have a combination that you like. Cut the swatches out and arrange them to see how they work together. If the colour palette isn't quite right, study the photo to see what colours could be missing and add those to your swatches. Continue in this manner until your colour scheme feels complete.

If you prefer to work digitally, photo-editing software, such as Photoshop, is a great tool to help you develop a colour palette in the same manner.

START WITH THE FABRIC

Choosing a singular printed fabric around which to build your colour palette is another option. In this case, the fabric's designer has already done the hard work and developed a concise colour scheme. Use the print's background and accent colours as a starting point from which to build your own palette. You can choose to match the colours in the print or you can pick other colours that will contrast with them. If you are attracted to a particular textile, you can use it as the inspiration for your colour palette even if you don't plan on using it in your quilt.

5: MATCHING FABRICS AND COLOURS

Today's quilters are lucky when it comes to the choices of fabric available. The range of prints and solids is vast – there really is something for everyone. Mixing and matching these fabrics into a quilt top is part of the fun. After all – what quilter doesn't like playing with fabric?

MATCHING SOLID COLOURS AND PRINTS

Choosing beautiful fabrics for a quilt project is one of the most satisfying parts of the process. For some, creating a visually balanced and interesting assortment of prints and solids is second nature. For others, though, it's downright terrifying. Whichever camp you belong in, if you keep a few simple things in mind, matching solids and prints will be fun and easy.

If you are working with a large-scale print, it's likely that it will contain many colours. Take a look at the fabric's selvedge. Those little numbered dots of colour represent all the colours present in the print. Probably the simplest way to find a solid colour that will match a printed fabric is to compare the solids with the dye marker dots. The colours do not need to be a perfect match, but they should blend and look pleasing to your eye. Some small-scale prints read as solids. These basic geometric, floral, and tone-on-tone prints will look like solid-coloured fabric from a few steps away and can be used accordingly in your quilt.

Simple prints that contain only two or three colours will work well with any solid that will highlight the print. You can choose a lighter or darker value of one of the colours to complement the print. Don't forget about contrasting colours, too. Sometimes the best match is a colour that isn't in the print, but one that contrasts with it. Try matching warm and cool colours for interesting combinations, or keep everything in the same temperature family – warms with warms and cools with cools – for a subtle effect.

Finally, remember the neutrals. Whites, off-whites, greys and browns come in many different shades. There's black, too. With the number of choices available, you should be able to find one or more neutrals that will work well with your prints and help to create a visually stimulating quilt.

Linen and Liberty baby quilt by Siobhan Rogers.

ASSESSING MATCHES
Place fabrics next to each other and take a few steps back. Sometimes putting a little distance between your eyes and the fabrics will help you determine whether they match or not.

COMBINING DIFFERENT PRINTS

A visually interesting quilt begins with a good selection of fabrics. Although it can be overwhelming to pull together a cohesive group of prints to use in your project, it is easily achieved if you keep a few things in mind.

LEARN FROM THE PROS
Look at a full line of designer quilting cottons. These fabrics are designed to work with one another and will cover a range of sizes and styles of prints in the same colour family. When combining fabrics for your quilt, you'll want to do the same thing: choose fabrics in a mix of patterns and colours with varying scales that all work well together.

START WITH A FOCUS FABRIC
When selecting prints, it is easiest to begin with a focus fabric. The focus fabric will give you a colour palette to work with and its style will help determine what other prints to pair with it.

DEFINE THE PALETTE

Select colours from the focus print and use these as a guideline for picking out other fabrics. Having a defined palette will help you keep the right balance between the colours in the quilt. Prints that share two of the colours in your quilt's palette will help carry the colour scheme across your project.

VARY THE PRINT STYLES

A good mix of pattern styles is what you are looking for. If the focus print is a large-scale, floral design, choosing some dots, checks, smaller florals and stripes to accompany it will add movement and interest to your quilt.

INCLUDE DIFFERENT SCALES

It's also important to vary the scale of the prints. Including various large-, medium- and small-scale patterns among the fabrics you choose will give the quilt more depth.

REPEAT MOTIFS

Look for some prints that are similar in style, but different in scale. The repetition of motifs in the same colour palette, but at different scales, helps create continuity and cohesion among your fabric choices.

ADD SOLIDS

Throwing a solid or two into your fabric mix will give your eyes a place to rest. You can also include tone-on-tone prints or other patterns that read as solids. These can be a neutral that will complement your other fabrics, such as white or grey, or a colour straight from the quilt's palette.

TRUST YOURSELF

It's easy to be overwhelmed when faced with multiple fabric choices. Sometimes it's best to walk away and come back to look at the fabrics with fresh eyes. Trust your intuition – you know what you like.

Opposite left: Lark patchwork by Meredith Daniel.
Opposite right: Pink linen quilt by Siobhan Rogers, long-arm quilted by Kim Bradley.
Above left: Warm Values quilt by Andi Herman.
Above right: Quilt for Maybelle by Andi Herman.

USING DIFFERENT TEXTURES

The easiest way to bring texture into a quilt is to use a variety of fabrics. With the myriad textiles available to contemporary quilters, it is not uncommon to combine different types of fabrics in a single quilt project. Doing this can create visual and tactile interest.

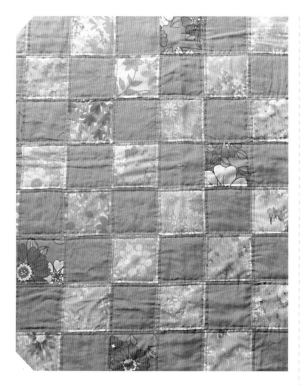

You can use different substrates of the same fibre to create texture in your project. For example, if you combine quilting cotton with silky smooth voile it will give parts of the quilt a 'toothier' feel than the rest. Using corduroy or cotton velveteen adds a soft, plush feeling that you cannot get from regular woven cotton. Another way to add texture to a quilt is to use fabrics made from different fibres. For example, pairing wool with linen would make for a cosy, soft quilt. Certainly, the options are as endless as the fabrics.

Using various fabrics as design elements is another way to incorporate texture into a quilt. Sprinkle the various textiles throughout the entire quilt or use them in a certain part of the design, such as in the sashing or borders. Make the quilt top from one kind of fabric, but the back from another. By carefully choosing how and where to use the different fabrics, you will have a unique, touchable quilt.

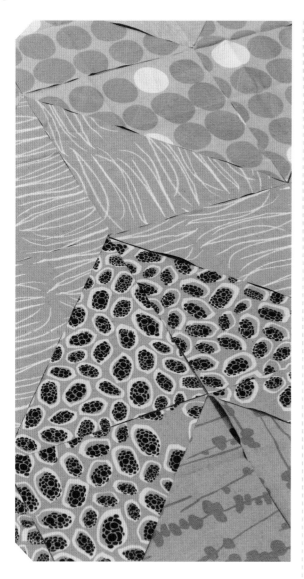

When working with different types of fabrics in the same quilt, it is important to consider how they will work together. You will get the best results if you are using fabrics of a similar weight. This will create less stress in the seams and also make quilting through different fibres easier. If you do decide to use fabrics of different weights together, take care when sewing them. You may need to increase the seam allowance to give it extra strength or interface lighter fabrics so that they will work well with heavier-weight ones.

Consider, too, how you will launder the quilt. If one of your fabrics is dry clean only, your entire quilt will have to be dry cleaned. Likewise, if all the fabrics are washable, pre-wash them in the same manner that you will launder them later before you start cutting and sewing. This will take care of any discrepancies in their shrinkage rates.

Opposite left: Linen and vintage fabric quilt by Andi Herman.
Opposite right: Granny square quilt by Jessica Fincham.
Above left: Cloth Zig Zag quilt by Siobhan Rogers, long-arm quilted by Kim Bradley.
Above right: Linen throw with appliqué patches by Siobhan Rogers.

BACKINGS AND BINDINGS

Choosing the backing and binding for your quilt is another chance to enhance the design of the quilt top.

BACKINGS

The quilt back is a crucial part of any quilting project. Determining what you want it to look like is part of the fun. Most quilt backs are pieced from one or more fabrics, as the variety of fabrics that are wider than 107 cm (42 in) is limited and they can be hard to find. Having a pieced backing gives you a multitude of design options. You can choose to make the backing out of one fabric or out of a few. When using more than one fabric, incorporating a strip of patchwork or extra quilt blocks into the back will tie its look to the quilt top nicely, and gives you a quilt that is beautiful on both sides.

Whether you use one or more fabrics, you can use a solid fabric or a print that is found in the quilt top. You can also choose a print that isn't seen anywhere else in the quilt, but that complements your colour palette. For a more contemporary look, think about using a solid-coloured fabric that contrasts with the front of the quilt. It might be fun to find a surprise like this on the quilt's reverse side.

BINDINGS

Like backings, bindings offer another chance to add a design element to the quilt. If you want a simple, contemporary look, you might choose a binding that matches the background of the quilt top. To draw attention to the binding, select a bold-coloured solid or print that complements the colour palette. A binding that contrasts can work well, too. Just think of how a graphic black and white quilt top would look framed by a pop of red or lime green.

When choosing the fabric for the binding, remember that you will only see a sliver of it around the edge of the quilt, and that it will look very different than the way it does on the bolt. Fold a small piece of potential binding fabric the same way that you will when you construct the binding, either on the bias or with the grain, and hold it next to the quilt top. Doing this will give you a good idea of what the binding will look like on your quilt before you cut and apply it.

Opposite left: Quilt for Maybelle by Andi Herman.
Opposite right: Scallop quilt by Meredith Daniel.
Clockwise from top left: Beehive quilt by Andi Herman;
Izzy's quilt by Andi Herman; Spinning Stars quilt by Meredith Daniel,
pattern by Anna Maria Horner.

ANNA MARIA HORNER

Nashville-based artist and author Anna Maria Horner designs vibrant and lush fabrics that are among the favourites of many contemporary quilters. Beyond fabric design, Anna Maria has a true love of sewing and making. This affinity for the handmade is evident in all she creates – quilts and patterns alike.

Anna Maria was introduced to hand sewing at a young age and progressed to the sewing machine when she got older. She particularly enjoyed sewing garments, making her own dresses for school dances and the like. She was introduced to patchwork and quilting during a mixed fibres class that she took in college while pursuing her fine art degree. While the class focused on techniques such as thread painting and weaving, it also included an exploration of colour theory. Armed with the formulas she learned in that class to create colour combinations, Anna Maria began her first quilting project. Despite the tedious cutting of its many pieces, she finished her kaleidoscope quilt and was eager to start another.

In fact, Anna Maria claims that her 'favourite quilt is always the NEXT quilt', as conceiving and developing a design then choosing which fabrics to use are the most exciting steps for her. She finds that quilting is a good mix of the left and right brain with creativity, planning, and maths all having their own place in the design process. Her process for choosing fabrics is dependent on whether she is making the quilt for personal use or to promote one of her fabric lines. When working with a particular fabric line, Anna Maria finds that the design becomes more about how to arrange the colour contained in the fabrics. Conversely, with personal quilts, her palette is slowly developed over time by grouping fabric, playing with prints and auditioning colours. Only then does she begin to think about the mechanics of the patchwork and how it will all come together.

Just as you would expect from a painter, Anna Maria's quilts are full of artistry. Both simple and complex at the same time, her quilts often contain interesting and fresh colour combinations, which she mixes together using straightforward shapes along with elements that give her designs movement. Like any other large-scale piece of fine art, Anna Maria considers composition and balance as she designs and she uses the quilt as a canvas, spontaneously responding to what she sees and adjusting the layout or arrangement as necessary. Every part of the quilt – the shapes, the fabrics, the quilting, the binding – works together to create a cohesive piece of work.

Anna Maria's quilt making is guided by the principle that 'more complicated is not necessarily more beautiful'. She advises quilters that 'looking at what you love, and figuring out why, then practising with your own materials, enough to become a master of your own tools, is all you need'.

Clockwise from top left: Petal Pusher; Feather Bed; Flight Map; Handquilt pillow; Garden Composition.

BLAIR STOCKER

Blair Stocker is a multi-crafting, Seattle-based artist who likes to make things. She blogs about the quilts she makes, paints and dreams about, among other creative pursuits, at Wise Craft.

Blair began crafting at an early age, but didn't learn to sew on a machine until she studied apparel design in college. At this point in her life, she realised that she truly loved making, bought a sewing machine and set about learning to use it. After her graduation, while working in apparel design in merchandising, she picked up even more technical sewing skills from watching the in-house sample sewers.

Quilting entered Blair's life after her daughter was born. Although she had always considered quilt making to be big and scary, she was inspired to give it a go after seeing a quilt made from baby clothes in a magazine. Blair was determined to complete a similar project, but her admitted lack of patience showed in the quilt's construction. With all its flaws, however, the quilt has become a well-loved treasure and in making it, Blair realised that quilting was a great creative outlet for her.

These days the quilts that Blair makes are mostly of her own design. She starts by sketching her ideas on graph paper and then adding colour. Recently she has begun to render her ideas in watercolour to play with different colour combinations. From these simple drawings and paintings, she develops her unique designs. She combines basic shapes in fresh, new ways, giving her projects a contemporary look, with a nod to traditional quilt making.

Blair is choosy about the fabrics she uses when she's sewing. She prefers vintage and secondhand prints, upcycled from men's shirts and women's skirts as well as feedsack fabrics. To complement these more interesting prints, she'll throw some solid cotton fabrics into the mix. Her quilts don't include sashing or borders as she likes to see the design 'fall off the edges of the quilt'. Blair pieces her projects on her home sewing machine and often quilts them by hand, not worrying too much about perfect stitches. She has recently begun exploring free-motion quilting and sometimes sends her work out to a long-arm quilter as well.

To say that Blair has come a long way from her first attempt at quilt making is an understatement. Her quilted projects are stunning, perfectly sewn works of functional art. She says, 'Quilts are beautiful; they have taught me so much about having patience, and I enjoy every part of the construction process. Some parts are exciting, some are meditative and repetitive, some are challenging, but it all has a beginning and ending point, and the result is beautiful and useful.'

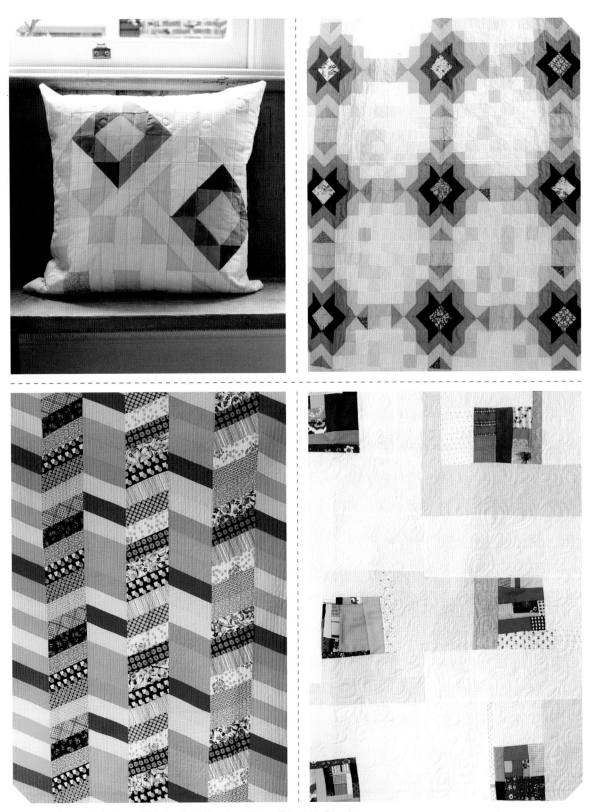

Clockwise from top left: Emerald Blocks; Echo Star; Jewel Boxes; Friendship Bracelet.

3

SECTION THREE
DESIGNS

❖ 6: SHAPES

Every quilt is made up of pieces, whether it's a few squares or an elaborate patchwork design of dozens of different shapes. Once you understand more about how different shapes are used in quilts and the most efficient ways of cutting, measuring and sewing them, you will be designing and making your own contemporary quilts in no time.

SQUARES AND RECTANGLES

Squares and rectangles are the primary shapes seen in quilts. They are simple, straightforward and extremely versatile. When paired with other shapes, they can form both basic and complex patterns.

TYPES

Squares have four sides all of equal length and four 90-degree angles. They are the foundation of the most basic quilt blocks.

Like squares, rectangles also have four 90-degree corners. Instead of four sides of equal length, though, they have two pairs of parallel sides of equal length Additionally, rectangles can be classified into two groups. 'True rectangles' are twice as long as they are wide. Rectangles that are more than twice as long as they are wide are called 'bars'. Both are used frequently in quilt blocks.

CUTTING AND MEASURING TIPS

Squares and rectangles are easily cut from strips of fabric. Begin with the finished measurement of your square or rectangle and add 13 mm (½ in) to account for seam allowances. Cut a strip of fabric to this length and cut squares and rectangles from it.

SEWING TIPS

With their straight sides, squares and rectangles are easy to sew. Their points and corners are easy to match and they are great for a beginner quilter to perfect sewing a straight 6 mm (¼ in) seam. Chain piecing these simple shapes is easy, too.

Top: Square patched quilt block by Erin Burke Harris.
Bottom: Squares quilt by Lydia Rudd.

TRIANGLES

Triangles are among the most frequently used shapes in quilting. They can be arranged and combined to form endless patterns.

TYPES

Equilateral triangles have three sides of equal length. Equilateral triangle pieces will have one side that is with the grain and two sides on the bias.

Half-square triangles are isosceles triangles – a square cut in half along the diagonal. The shorter sides are cut with the grain and the longer side is cut on the bias.

Quarter-square triangles are one quarter of a square that has been cut diagonally. They are isosceles triangles. The shorter sides are cut on the bias, and the long side is cut with the grain.

Long triangles are right scalene triangles. They have three sides of different lengths and one right angle. They are cut along the diagonal of a rectangle. The two sides adjacent to the right angle are cut with the grain of the fabric and the other side is on the bias.

Top: Half-square triangle. **Middle:** Quarter-square triangle. **Bottom:** Long triangle. All quilt blocks by Erin Burke Harris.

CUTTING AND MEASURING TIPS

For equilateral triangles, begin with the finished measurement of one side and add 19 mm (¾ in). Cut a strip of fabric to this length. Align the ruler along the top of the strip at the 60-degree mark and cut along it. This will then establish the first side of the triangle. Rotate the ruler so that its edge forms a point with the first cut and the 60-degree mark is in line with the fabric's bottom edge. Again, cut along the ruler's long edge. Continue rotating the ruler to cut more triangles.

For half-square triangles, cut a square that is 22 mm (⅞ in) longer and wider than the finished triangle's short sides. Cut the square in half diagonally.

Quarter-square triangles are cut from squares that are 32 mm (1¼ in) longer and wider than the short sides of the finished triangle. Cut the square in half twice diagonally.

To cut long triangles, you need to know the finished measurements of the sides adjacent to the right angle. Add 17 mm (¹¹⁄₁₆ in) to the shorter of these measurements and 8 mm (⁵⁄₁₆ in) to the longer. Cut a rectangle to these new measurements and then cut it diagonally.

SEWING TIPS

All triangles have at least one side that is cut on the bias. It is important not to stretch the bias edge as you sew –using spray starch can help to stabilise your fabric.

When sewing triangles together, you must align them properly along the seam line. Often, the points of the triangle will overlap the edges by 6 mm (¼ in). Pressing the seams open instead of to the side may make for a neater block.

Top left: Kaleidoscope quilt by Melissa Robinson.
Top right: Arielle's quilt by Karen Lewis.

❖ DIAMONDS

Like triangles, diamonds are frequently used in quilting. They work well in all sorts of arrangements and with other shapes.

TYPES

In quilts, diamonds are often squares that have been rotated 45 degrees and set on point. These diamonds have sides of equal lengths, cut with the straight grain, and 90-degree angles.

Another diamond often used in quilting is a rhombus. Similar to squares, rhombuses have sides of equal lengths, but two pairs of parallel sides. Instead of 90-degree interior angles, these diamonds have 30- or 45-degree angles at their sharpest points. Two sides are cut on the bias and two cut with the grain.

CUTTING AND MEASURING TIPS

Diamonds are typically cut using a rotary cutter and a straight quilter's ruler. Strips are cut from the width of the fabric and then further cut into diamonds.

Square diamonds set on point are cut in the same manner as squares. Add 13 mm (½ in) to the finished measurement of the square. Cut a strip of fabric to this measurement and cut squares from the strip.

Rhombus diamonds can be cut by using the angle markings on the quilting ruler. The distance between the parallel edges of the finished diamond will determine its size. Cut a strip of fabric that is 13 mm longer than this measurement. Using the markings on the ruler, line up the appropriate angle with the bottom edge of the fabric. Cut along the long side of the ruler to establish the diamond's edge. Next, measure the cutting height of the diamond from this edge. Cut along the long edge of the ruler to yield one diamond. Use the new angled edge on the strip as your established edge and continue cutting in this manner.

SEWING TIPS

Square diamonds set on point are sewn together in strips. The strips are then arranged diagonally to get the desired effect.

Diamonds that have two sides with bias edges may stretch when you are sewing them. Use lots of pins or spray starch your fabric before you cut your shapes to avoid this. To make sure the points match up correctly, diamonds must be aligned along the seam line, with points overlapping.

Some quilt patterns have diamonds that are sewn together to form intricate shapes, such as stars or flowers. These may need to be hand or paper pieced if you want to avoid machine sewing inset Y-seams.

Opposite left: Sunkissed Diamond quilt by traceyjay quilts.
Top left: Rhomboid diamond shapes by Erin Burke Harris.
Top right: Square diamond shape by Erin Burke Harris.

 # HEXAGONS

Hexagons are six-sided figures with equal sides that can fit together without space between them. When cut from a strip of fabric, they have one set of parallel edges cut with the grain and two sets of parallel edges on the bias.

CUTTING AND MEASURING TIPS

Hand-pieced hexagons are often cut using a finished-sized paper template. The template is pinned to the fabric and cut out 6 mm (¼ in) bigger than the original template to create a seam allowance. This method is great for fussy-cutting hexagons to showcase a particular part of a print.

Hexagons can also be cut using a rotary cutter and ruler. Make a template that includes a 6 mm (¼ in) seam allowance, and cut strips of fabric that width. Trace the template so that the top and the bottom are flush with the fabric's edges and the sides of the traced hexagons meet at the points. Using your ruler, cut 'X's along the traced lines. Specialist quilting rulers make cutting hexagons fast and easy.

SEWING TIPS

Hexagons are most often pieced by hand, using the English paper piecing technique (see page 146). Once sewn into groups, they may be appliquéd onto a backing fabric. They can be pieced by machine, although this is a bit trickier. Maintaining an exact 6 mm (¼ in) seam allowance and taking your time is essential to mastering inset Y-seams.

CIRCLES AND CURVED SHAPES

Circles and curved shapes add design impact to quilts' predominantly straight lines.

CUTTING AND MEASURING TIPS

Most curved shapes are cut using a template. If you are cutting a curved shape that has a straight edge, often – but not always – it will be aligned with the grain of the fabric to minimise stretching. It's very important to pay close attention to the pattern you are using and align any grain markings accordingly.

SEWING TIPS

Many sewers fear curves, but they are easy to sew if you take your time and use a lot of pins. Start pinning in the middle and at the ends of the piece, easing the rest of the fabric so it lies flat. Sew slowly, making sure you maintain a 6 mm (¼ in) seam allowance.

Opposite top: Hexagon shapes by Erin Burke Harris.
Opposite bottom: DUDQS12 quilt by Lydia Rudd.
Top left: Drunkard's Path quilt by Erin Burke Harris.
Top right: Circles quilt by Clare Mansell.

◆ 7: QUILT BLOCKS

Both the well-established layouts of traditional quilt blocks and the less structured modern versions have their place in the contemporary quilter's arsenal. Exploring the origins of these different blocks will help you understand the elements that are important in contemporary quilt designs. From there, you can choose what to include in – or even leave out of – your quilting projects to realise your own creative vision.

◆ TRADITIONAL BLOCKS

Traditional quilt blocks have stood the test of time. They are tried and true patterns that quilters have used for many years and return to again and again.

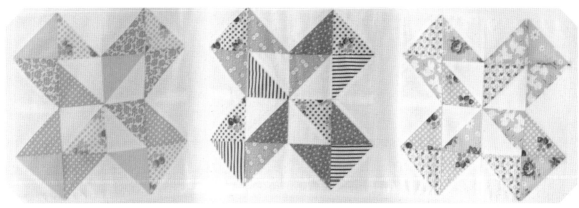

CHARACTERISTICS

The most common traditional quilt blocks are often geometric, based on a grid comprised of squares. Other traditional blocks do not follow this pattern, and have various shapes pieced in a symmetrical fashion. If sewn together without sashing between them, traditional quilt blocks often display a larger, overall pattern.

Most traditional blocks use printed fabrics and have little negative space. The negative space that does exist is often seen in the background fabric or as sashing and borders around traditional blocks. Solid fabrics are used, but it is not uncommon to see tone-on-tone prints that suggest solid colour in their place. Colour palettes may be limited to a few specific colours or a certain type of colour, such as pastels or bright, primary tones.

Traditional blocks are orderly and precisely made. They may be hand or machine sewn, and follow well-established piecing methods. Seams are 6 mm (¼ in) and pressed to the side. When sewn together, the seam lines all match and points are evident.

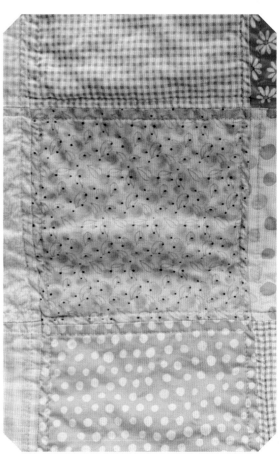

Top: Dutch Pinwheel quilt by Jessica Fincham.
Above: Patchwork quilt by Katherine Codega.

TYPES

Grid-based quilt blocks can generally be divided into four main layouts. Four-patch blocks are made from four individual squares laid out in a 2 × 2 grid. Nine-patch blocks have a 3 × 3 grid. The finished size of these blocks is often 15, 30 or 45 cm (6, 12 or 18 in).

Five-patch and seven-patch blocks are laid out in grids that are 5 × 5 and 7 × 7 respectively. Five-patch blocks quite often have a finished measurement of 25 cm (10 in) while seven-patch blocks are generally 36 cm (14 in).

The individual squares within these larger blocks may be pieced from different, smaller shapes. These blocks may also combine one or more squares in the grid to make larger squares, triangles, diamonds and rectangles.

Other traditional quilt blocks do not fall into the patch and grid category. They have small shapes pieced together to form a larger block. Some examples are the Log Cabin and Double Wedding Ring patterns.

APPLICATIONS

Now, modern-day quilters have the opportunity to use traditional blocks in more fun and exciting ways. Some options include giving a contemporary colour palette to a classic pattern for a fresher, new look. Use graphic, modern prints and solid-coloured fabrics for a modern approach. Play with scale by supersizing or shrinking blocks.

Top: Four patch block. **Middle:** Seven patch block.
Bottom: Five patch block. All blocks by Erin Burke Harris.

Top: Ollalieberry quilt by Katherine Codega, based on a pattern by Alicia Paulson.
Above left: Marmalade baby quilt by Debbie Homick. **Above right:** Zooey quilt by Lucrecia Hale.

MODERN BLOCKS

Modern quilt blocks are based on traditional quilting ideas – but they break all the rules. Interesting colour combinations, different shapes and innovative use of prints make these quilt blocks fresh and exciting.

CHARACTERISTICS

The number one rule of modern quilting is that there are no rules. That said, most modern quilt blocks stem directly from traditional ones. The differences between the two can be slight or extreme. It may be the current colour palette and contemporary prints that make a block modern. Or the twist could be an increased use of solid colours or more negative space than you'd see in traditional blocks. Modern quilt blocks often use white and grey as neutrals, with crisp, clear colours. They often reimagine traditional blocks by changing the proportions of the shapes or skewing the straight lines slightly. Some modern blocks do not have a visible structure. Additionally, textiles other than quilter's cotton may be used alone or along with other fibres. The possibilities are endless.

Modern blocks are sewn using a variety of methods. They are generally machine sewn with 6 mm (¼") seams, using traditional piecing methods. They may also include improvisational piecing or wonky lines. Most modern quilters use tried and true quilting methods, adapting them to suit their needs. And when traditional piecing and sewing do not fit the bill, modern quilters use innovative methods to realise their visions.

Top: Single Girl quilt by Melissa Robinson, pattern by Denyse Schmidt.
Bottom: Nina quilt by Lucrecia Hale.

APPLICATIONS

Every modern quilter approaches sewing with a different perspective and, consequently, modern blocks are as limitless as the imagination. Their applications in modern quilts are just as endless. Variations of the same block will often be used throughout a quilt top. By changing one aspect from block to block, such as the colours or size, you can achieve a cohesive, modern quilt. Modern blocks can be floated individually or in small groupings on a larger background to achieve a minimalist look that is not seen with traditional blocks. Think about symmetry, or the lack of it, when making modern blocks. The blocks themselves may be asymmetrical, or perhaps pieced together in a way that results in an asymmetrical quilt. These are just some ideas to jump-start your own creativity. With modern blocks, there is no end to your options.

Cloth Zig Zag quilt by Siobhan Rogers.

MIXING AND MATCHING QUILT BLOCKS

With the myriad quilt blocks out there, you have many options when planning your quilt. You can choose to repeat the same block or mix a bunch of different blocks together. Whether you are using traditional blocks, modern blocks or a combination of the two, by following a few guidelines, you can successfully mix and match quilt blocks with ease.

USING ONE TYPE OF BLOCK

Many quilts consist of one block repeated over the quilt top. To make this approach more contemporary, plan on making variations to the chosen quilt block. You can do this in a few different ways. The most obvious is to choose a cohesive colour palette of three or more colours. Keep the background fabric the same and use different prints in your palette to make the blocks unique. Or consider using just two or three colours from your palette for each block, varying the colour combinations from block to block. When sewn together, the entire palette will be seen across the quilt. Another option is to rotate your blocks so that they are oriented differently instead of facing all the same direction. This will create visual interest and give movement to your quilt top.

+X quilt by Melissa Robinson.

USING MORE THAN ONE
TYPE OF BLOCK

If you are planning on using more than one type of block in your quilt, you need to keep one part of it consistent throughout. You could do this by having a distinct colour palette or a particular fabric used throughout that ties all the differing blocks together. You could also focus on a certain design element or shape for cohesiveness. Maybe each block could be a different star, or have a certain colour in its centre, for example. Finally, you need to consider proportion. Uniform sizing in the varying blocks is key to mixing them together successfully. It's also important to consider scale. If most of your blocks have pieces of similar size, they are much more likely to look good together than a grouping of pieces that range from extra-large to tiny.

Top: Farmer's Wife quilt by Mary E. Goodwin, pattern by Laurie Hird.
Bottom: Sophie's quilt by Andi Herman, quilted by Susan Campbell of Rowdy Flat Quilting.

◆ 8: BLOCK LAYOUTS AND SETTINGS

You've chosen your shapes and planned your blocks. The next step in designing your quilt is deciding how to arrange the individual quilt blocks into a well-balanced and cohesive design. Learning about the different quilt settings is a great place to begin. With straightforward guidelines, these traditional layouts provide you with a variety of options to develop your individual traditional and contemporary quilt designs.

◆ SIDE-BY-SIDE SETTINGS

When laying out quilt blocks, there are many options to choose from. The most commonly used setting for quilts is the side-by-side or straight setting.

CHARACTERISTICS

In straight settings, the quilt blocks are laid out in horizontal and vertical rows without any sashing between them. The quilt blocks are all the same size and are laid out in a grid. The blocks can be all the same pattern and colours or a variety of different designs and fabrics.

APPLICATIONS

In traditional quilts, where identical blocks of the same pattern and fabrics are used, the side-by-side layout often reveals a secondary pattern over the quilt top. Additional patterns also emerge when some quilt blocks are rotated by 90 or 180 degrees and are laid out in a straight setting.

The same quilt block does not have to be used repeatedly in a side-by-side setting, but the blocks do need to be of uniform size. Many contemporary quilts, even those with improvisational piecing, have straight settings. It may be harder to distinguish the seam lines due to the use of more solid-coloured fabrics and asymmetrical shapes, but the original grid structure is still there.

Googly Eyes by Lucrecia Hale.

PROS

Side-by-side settings are very straightforward and easy to construct. They work well for both traditional and modern quilt designs.

CONS

More intricate quilt squares laid out in a straight setting may make for a very busy quilt top.

HORIZONTAL AND VERTICAL SETTINGS

In horizontal and vertical settings, blocks are set end to end horizontally or vertically across a quilt.

CHARACTERISTICS

Unlike with straight settings, horizontal and vertical settings are not laid out in a grid. Instead these settings contain quilt blocks that are lined up parallel to each other along a horizontal or vertical plane. The quilt may contain one row of blocks with negative space on either end or multiple rows separated by sashing or fabric strips. Blocks may also be laid out in a half-drop pattern, like bricks, without the seams matching at the corners.

When using a horizontal setting, the blocks in each row should be the same height, but may vary in width. For vertical settings, the opposite is true: the blocks are the same width, but they may be different heights.

Top: Pow Wow quilt by Melissa Robinson, pattern by Cluck Cluck Sew.
Bottom: Sanctuary Squares by Cindy Lammon.

APPLICATIONS

Strip quilts are good examples of horizontal and vertical settings. Lengths of fabric are sewn together in strips, from side to side or up and down, creating either horizontal or vertical stripes.

Separating rows of quilt blocks with sashing is another way to utilise horizontal and vertical settings. Using solid fabrics on either side of a row of blocks will create negative space that will highlight a small group of quilt squares. Laying blocks out in a more brick-like pattern along horizontal or vertical planes creates a contemporary look for a quilt made from traditional quilt blocks.

PROS

Horizontal and vertical settings can use asymmetry to give a quilt a modern look. Because it is not crucial that the blocks meet at their corners, it is easy to combine blocks of similar height but unequal width using a horizontal setting, or blocks of similar width but different height in a vertical setting.

CONS

These settings do not work well for traditional quilt blocks that create a secondary pattern when grouped together en masse. They are also not suited to square quilt blocks unless they are laid out as bricks with broken joints or the rows are separated with sashing.

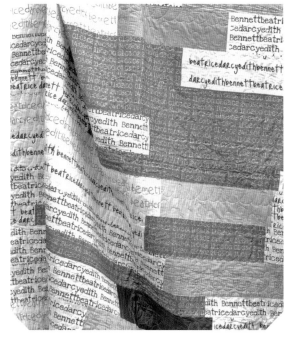

Top: Liberty Love Scraps baby quilt by Siobhan Rogers.
Bottom: Text Quilt Monochromatic by Siobhan Rogers.

✖ DIAGONAL AND ON-POINT SETTINGS

In diagonal settings, the quilt blocks are set on point so that the squares appear as diamonds.

CHARACTERISTICS

The quilt blocks are laid out diagonally and setting triangles are added along the sides of the rows and at the corners to fill in the gaps and make the quilt top edges straight. Rows are sewn diagonally, starting with the side setting triangles. The diagonal rows are lined up at their seams and then sewn together. The corner setting triangles are added last.

APPLICATIONS

Many traditional quilt blocks were designed to be seen as diamonds and look best when set on point. Other blocks work well when oriented straight or on the diagonal. In these instances, whether you use an on-point setting is a matter of personal preference.

Setting triangles must be used to fill in the spaces at the ends of diagonal rows. These can be pieced blocks that are cut to fit the gaps or a single fabric cut to size. Because it's important that the quilt edges are with the fabric's grain and not on the bias, corner setting triangles are always half-square triangles and side setting pieces are quarter-square triangles.

PROS

On-point settings work well with traditional quilt blocks. Using an updated colour palette will give them a contemporary feel. A diagonal layout also works well with added sashing and borders.

CONS

Setting triangles with bias edges may stretch and be difficult to sew. For this reason, it is important that the triangles are cut with their outer edges aligned with the fabric's grain.

Opposite: Shadow Star quilt by Rita Hodge. **Above:** Make a Wish quilt by Emma How.

✖ ALTERNATING SETTINGS

Imagine a chess board with red and black squares. In quilt form, the red-black-red-black layout is known as an alternating setting.

CHARACTERISTICS

Two quilt blocks, laid out one after the other, make an alternating setting. These blocks can be plain squares of two different fabrics or two different patchwork blocks. You can also alternate patchwork blocks and plain squares in this type of setting. The key is that you have two blocks and that they succeed one another in turn.

APPLICATIONS

Alternating settings that are laid out side-by-side are referred to as 'alternating straight settings' and have the same characteristics as other straight settings. These quilts are laid out just as a chess board is, with the alternating squares arranged in horizontal and vertical rows.

Similarly, quilts with alternating blocks on the diagonal are called 'alternating on-point settings'. Blocks in these quilts alternate across the diagonal row. When you look at the quilt straight on, blocks of the same pattern appear like diamonds in horizontal rows touching at their points.

When using two alternating pieced blocks, a larger overall pattern may be revealed across the quilt. Many traditional quilt patterns are designed this way. If you use plain blocks alongside patchwork blocks, think carefully about the fabrics you choose. Plain blocks in the same fabric as the background of the pieced blocks will create a different look than if you use a contrasting print or different coloured fabric.

PROS

Alternating settings with plain and patchwork blocks combined have more space around the pieced blocks, allowing them to stand out. Using alternating plain blocks is time-saving as there is less cutting and piecing to accomplish.

CONS

The overall design of the quilt may suffer if you choose patchwork squares that are too busy when alternated. Using too many alternating plain squares, however, may result in a rather lacklustre-looking quilt.

Polar Bear quilt by Rita Hodge.

MEDALLION SETTINGS

A traditional quilting design, medallion settings have been around for hundreds of years. With a central motif and multiple borders, this type of quilt lends itself to both traditional and contemporary variations.

CHARACTERISTICS

At the centre of the medallion setting is a large quilt block. Typically pieced or appliquéd, this initial square serves as the first block in a medallion setting. The medallion is surrounded by two or more borders, which are consistent with the theme of the central motif. The borders may be single pieces of fabric, but are often patchwork or appliqué, and can vary in width. The resulting quilt is square with sides of equal lengths.

APPLICATIONS

Medallion settings are a wonderful way to highlight an intricate patchwork or appliqué design. The key is to maintain a cohesive look by repeating shapes and motifs throughout the quilt's borders. It is wise to plan the design in advance and to use a consistent colour scheme throughout. Choose a colour palette and variety of fabrics, prints and solids, in these tones. Make sure that you have enough of each fabric before you begin cutting and sewing. For a modern-looking medallion quilt, use a generous amount of solids and other graphic prints. If you have a special piece of fabric sitting in your stash, think about using it as the centre square in a medallion quilt. It would be a wonderful way to showcase a favourite textile.

PROS

With multiple borders, a medallion setting is a great way to try different piecing methods, new-to-you sewing techniques and a variety of different shapes in one project.

CONS

A well-planned medallion setting requires a good amount of figuring to ensure the borders are the right sizes. If maths isn't your thing, use an existing medallion pattern instead of designing one yourself.

Opposite and above: Medallion quilt made by Beatrice Forrer on a course with Sara Cook.

ONE-PATCH SETTINGS

The repetition of one simple shape in various patterns and colours makes one-patch quilts look more complex than they really are.

CHARACTERISTICS

One-patch quilt settings are constructed from a single repeating shape that interlocks without spaces across the quilt top.

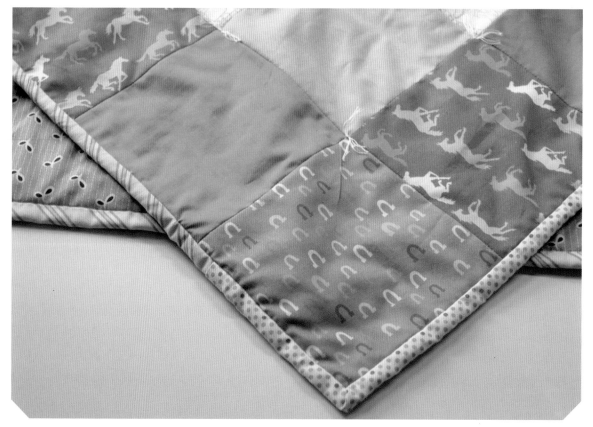

APPLICATIONS

Quilts with one-patch settings can be made from all kinds of different shapes. Squares, hexagons and equilateral triangles are commonly used for one-patch quilts. These shapes all have sides of equal length, making them easy to lay out in an interlocking fashion. Isosceles and right-angled triangles as well as rectangles, diamonds and kites are also geometric shapes that interlock nicely in a one-patch setting. However, because these shapes have sides of varying lengths, they may need to be rotated to fit together without spaces between them.

Because many of the shapes used in one-patch settings do not have square corners, the edges of the quilt top will be uneven. It is perfectly acceptable to use partial patches to fill these spaces so that the resulting quilt will have straight sides. Using partial shapes won't alter the quilt's one-patch designation.

Some well-known one-patch settings include Grandmother's Garden made from hexagons, Tumbling Blocks made from parallelograms, and Thousand Pyramids made from equilateral triangles. All of these designs uses colour and fabric placement to reveal a larger pattern over the quilt top. For a contemporary take on these traditional patterns, consider using only solid fabrics or a limited colour palette. Super-size the scale of the patch for another modern variation on a one-patch setting.

PROS

One-patch quilts contain one shape, making them easy to plan and cut. Their patterns are graphic, so they lend themselves to traditional and contemporary interpretations.

CONS

Some one-patch shapes such as hexagons and diamonds require set-in or Y-seams that are not easily machine-pieced.

Opposite top: Grandmother's Flower Garden by Andi Herman.
Opposite bottom: Giddy Up quilt by Katherine Codega.
Above: Patchwork quilt by Katherine Codega.

◆ 9: STYLES AND ARRANGEMENTS

Different forms of sewing and quilting have been around for hundreds of years. Looking at some of the different styles of quilting and where they came from gives a broader context for understanding what quilting today is all about. From simple patchwork designs to modern artistic interpretations, there is sure to be one or more quilting styles that will inspire you in your creative work.

◆ TRADITIONAL PATCHWORK

Today's patchwork quilts have their roots in the mid-1800s, when women began to make pieced quilts from fabric left over from clothing. Traditionally made from wool, linen and chintz, the first quilts were designed around a centre medallion with pieced borders that contained individual quilt blocks. Crazy quilts, made from oddly shaped bits of fabric and embellished with embroidery, were another popular form.

CHARACTERISTICS

Patchwork quilts consist of pieced blocks that are often sewn together in a grid formation. The blocks in each quilt may be all the same pattern or a sampler of different patterns. Typical patchwork quilts can range in size from small dolls' quilts and decorative wall hangings to larger, bed-sized quilts.

TYPES OF FABRICS

Then: The first patchwork quilts were made from wool, linen and coated chintz. Gradually, as woven cotton became more readily available, it grew to be the most common textile in quilts.

Now: Quilter's cotton remains the predominant choice when making traditionally inspired patchwork quilts today. However, the large variety of textiles commercially available allows quilters to have more options. Cotton substrates and linen, silk and lightweight wools are also good choices for modern variations of traditional patchwork quilting.

TYPES OF BLOCKS AND DESIGNS

Some traditional patchwork quilts are samplers that have a variety of different blocks in similar colours. These blocks often contain simple geometric shapes that form pictorial images. They might also feature different blocks of a similar technique. In sampler quilts, the blocks are frequently separated by sashing fabric and often surrounded by borders along the perimeter. Other traditional patchwork blocks are solely geometric. When sewn together without

Creamsicle quilt by Katherine Codega.

sashing, they then showcase an overall pattern. Depending on how the blocks are rotated and placed, the overall design can vary. By using different colour values in the patchwork, quilters can change the entire look of the quilt.

TYPES OF COLOURS

Then: Traditional patchwork quilts were made in all colours. From the early twentieth century, brighter tones and pastel colours were used more often.

Now: Today quilters have immense flexibility when it comes to colour. Deep, saturated colours and light, airy pastels create a modern look. Neutral colours can highlight brights or be subtle companions to lighter tones. Varying shades of a single colour creates a modern look.

JAPANESE SASHIKO QUILTS

Japan has been home to a rich quilting tradition for hundreds of years. As with other cold-climate countries, quilting evolved from a need for layered warmth in clothing and in bedding.

CHARACTERISTICS

Many antique and contemporary Japanese quilts showcase sashiko stitching. This running stitch is longer than a typical American hand quilting stitch and is made using loosely twisted, heavier thread. Sashiko is sewn in repeating and interlocking graphic patterns with a needle that has a large enough eye to accommodate the thick thread. Good substitutions for sashiko thread can include perle cotton and four strands of embroidery thread.

TYPES OF FABRICS

Then: The earliest Japanese quilts were futons. These multi-layered sleeping pallets and their covers were made of layers of cotton, hemp and other plant fibres that were sewn together. Silk fabric was used, but only for the highest classes and nobility.

Now: Contemporary Japanese quilts are similar to their Western counterparts. They contain fabrics that are commercially available, such as cotton, silk and linen.

TYPES OF BLOCKS AND DESIGNS

Then: Sashiko stitching was decorative, but utilitarian at the same time. It was used to reinforce fabrics for wear as well as to tack layers of fabric together for warmth. Stitching patterns were derived from nature and traditional symbols.

Now: Sashiko stitching is still practised in Japan as a quilting stitch and as decorative embroidery. Traditional patterns continue to be used as well as graphic designs that incorporate the use of negative space. Contemporary Japanese quilters also favour patchwork and appliqué quilting, similar to the American tradition.

TYPES OF COLOURS

Then: The indigo plant was widespread throughout Japan and used to dye fabrics. Colours ranged from the darkest inky blues to lighter sky tones. To create contrast with the blue fabrics, most sashiko stitching was done with white or light, natural-coloured, threads.

Now: Sashiko stitching is still frequently seen as lighter thread on a darker ground and sometimes in the reverse with darker stitches on a lighter fabric. Contrasting colours and subtle monochromatic values can be used for a more contemporary take on this traditional stitching method.

Top: Sashiko Angles by Saké Puppets. **Bottom left:** Indigo Arc wholecloth. **Bottom right:** Sashiko-inspired Alabama quilt. Both by Folk Fibers.

❖ HAWAIIAN QUILTS

Before the introduction of cotton cloth to Hawaii by Western explorers in the mid-1800s, quilting did not exist there. American missionaries taught Hawaiian women hand needlework, including patchwork and appliqué. With their new skills and the greater accessibility of large pieces of fabric, Hawaiian quilters adapted their traditional bed coverings into what are known today as Hawaiian quilts.

CHARACTERISTICS

Hawaiian quilts have large, radially symmetrical motifs that are often inspired by nature. These motifs are brightly coloured and appliquéd to the base cloth by hand. The appliqué piece is cut from a folded cloth in the same way as you would cut a paper snowflake, and is then hand sewn to the base cloth. After the appliqué is completed, the quilts are finished with outline and echo hand quilting. Typically Hawaiian quilts contain two colours – one for the background and one for the appliqué piece.

TYPES OF FABRICS AND COLOURS

Then: Contemporary Hawaiian quilts evolved from a traditional Hawaiian bed covering called kapa. Fibres from mulberry trees were pounded into a fabric. The fabrics were layered into a bed covering, the top layer of which was decorated with large painted or dyed botanical motifs.

Now: Following the tradition of the decorated kapa, Hawaiian quilts are constructed with solid-coloured cotton fabrics. A bright, vivid colour is often used for the appliqué piece, which is then sewn to a white or light-coloured background fabric.

TYPES OF DESIGNS

Then: Legend says that the first Hawaiian quilt was inspired by the shadow of a breadfruit tree on a piece of fabric. Whether this is true or not, the motifs often do resemble flowers or nature-inspired silhouettes. They are large in size, typically covering the entire quilt top.

Now: The appliqué motifs used in Hawaiian quilts continue to be bold and graphic. In addition to the large, symmetrical design in the centre of the quilt, smaller appliqué pieces are sometimes added in the corners.

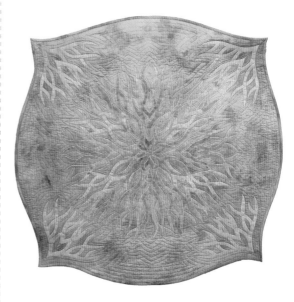

Haleakala Sunrise quilt by Sarah Ann Smith.

Top: Hawaiian quilt by Sara Cook. **Bottom:** Haleakala Sunrise Dragon's Breath by Sarah Ann Smith.

PROVENÇAL QUILTS

Unlike their American counterparts, traditional French Provençal quilts were not made from multiple fabrics in patchwork and appliqué designs. Instead, French quilters made elaborate whole cloth quilts, beginning as early as the 17th century.

CHARACTERISTICS

Boutis, as Provençal quilts are often called, consist of two layers of fabric. A design is transferred to the top fabric and then the two layers are sewn together by hand using a small running stitch. Once the design's outline has been completely sewn, cotton cording or wadding is stuffed between the layers of fabric using a long needle to give the quilt depth.

Other Provençal whole cloth quilts were made of three layers, just as traditional American quilts are. They have cotton, wool or silk for wadding and are covered on each side with plain or printed fabric.

TYPES OF FABRICS

Then: The first Provençal quilts had a high-quality fabric for the top layer and loosely woven, lesser-quality fabric for the back layer. Made mostly from cotton, linen or silk, eventually finer fabrics were used for both sides, making the quilt reversible.

Now: Due to its time-consuming method, boutis are not widely made these days. The artisans who do continue this practice use very lightweight fabrics such as cotton batiste. Other contemporary French quilters have been influenced by the American patchwork quilting tradition and use a variety of fabrics in their quilts, especially cotton, linen, wool and silk.

TYPES OF DESIGNS

Both boutis and the other whole cloth Provençal quilts contain intricate quilting designs that are inspired by nature, such as flowers, oak leaves, animals and fruit. Religious symbols, initials and dates were included in boutis and whole cloth quilts made for special occasions such as weddings.

TYPES OF COLOURS

Then: Traditional boutis were made from solid-coloured fabrics, whereas the other whole cloth quilts could have prints and/or solids. The most traditional colours were white, red, gold and indigo.

Now: The quilters that take the time to make boutis generally use white or other light-coloured fabrics. Other modern French quilts feature a range of colours, from bright, saturated shades to lighter pastels and everything in between.

Top: Waratah Rhythms by Annie London.
Bottom: French Tulips by Annie London.

OTHER TYPES OF QUILTS

AMISH QUILTS

The Amish community are a religious group, founded by German immigrants to Pennsylvania. They reject modern technology, such as electricity and motorised transport, preferring to live a simple life, without any unnecessary adornment.

Traditionally, quilts were made purely for practical reasons or as part of a woman's dowry, but now Amish quilts are collectors items and are valued as works of art around the world due to their high quality. The quilts were made from leftover scraps of fabric, which were typically dark colours, such as blues, purples, greens and reds. Modern Amish quilts do have brighter colours. Cotton and wool fabrics are mainly used, in plain colours, rather than patterns. They feature intricate, geometrical designs, often with a single, central motif and a black border.

NATIVE AMERICAN STAR QUILTS

During the late 19th century, missionaries taught Native American girls to quilt. The result was the star quilts, mostly associated with the Plains Indians. After learning the quilting techniques, they developed their own distinctive style, with a central star motif formed from diamond-shaped pieces. These quilts included similar designs to the ones that had traditionally been painted on buffalo hides, and had ceremonial and spiritual purposes, as well as practical ones.

 # ART QUILTS

Simply put, art quilting is the process of using traditional quilting techniques to create a piece of art. As such, art quilts contain at least two layers of fabric that are stitched together, with the stitches spreading across the entire work. These pieces are not necessarily intended to function as quilts. Instead, they are art that is intended to hang on a wall or be viewed as a soft sculpture.

Art quilting has an aesthetic sensibility consistent with other visual arts. Just as painters use paint, art quilters are artists who choose to use fabric and thread as their primary media. Art quilters reflect on their own experiences and develop ideas to create unique designs instead of relying on traditional quilt blocks and patterns as the basis for their work.

Some art quilts are constructed using traditional piecing and quilting techniques, whereas many others don't conform to well-established quilting rules. Each artist uses the methods most suited to the realisation of their vision and consequently both hand stitching and machine sewing are used in the assembly of these quilts. Free-motion machine stitching and embroidery are just some of the sewn embellishments used for surface design.

Art quilting is a broad term and accordingly, sewing is not the only technique used when creating art quilts. Manipulating fabrics with dyes and paints is common, as are stamping and stencilling. Appliqué can be used to add layers of fabrics as well as three-dimensional objects such as beads and trims to the quilt top. Additionally, art quilters use a wide range of textiles in their work. Instead of being limited by quilter's cottons, these artists employ silks, wools, felt, linen and even sheer fabrics like organza to bring their artistic vision to fruition. Some artists will even include unconventional materials such as paper and plastic in their quilts.

Wicked Witch of the East by Sara Cook.

Clockwise from top left: Winter Forest quilt by Frieda Anderson; SunSet Pines by Frieda Anderson; Wicked Witch of the West by Sara Cook.

✦ COLLAGE QUILTS

Just like paper collages, collage quilts contain a variety of materials and embellishments that might not necessarily relate to one another, but that in a single work of art join to tell a story.

CHARACTERISTICS

This form of art quilting is constructed in the same manner as a traditional quilt with a top, wadding and backing. The quilt top may contain various different techniques, and surface designs including piecing, appliqué, layering and embellishing. The layers are held together with either machine or hand quilting and the resulting quilt is often hung on the wall instead of being used in a traditional manner.

MATERIALS USED

Photography is one medium used in paper collage that is also integral to collage quilts. With a home computer, art quilters are able to print photographs onto transfer papers that can be ironed onto fabric for use in the quilt. Additionally, specialist fabric sheets for use in inkjet printers are available to purchase at quilt and fabric stores.

As with most art quilters, it is common for collage quilters to use a variety of textiles in their work. Combining traditional quilting cottons with textured silks, wools and linens gives collage quilts increased depth and interest. Using fabrics with sentimental value, such as small pieces from treasured clothing or the logo from a favourite t-shirt, creates personal meaning in the finished work. A variety of different embellishments, such as paints, trims, beads and embroidery, can be added as extra details to enhance the piece and to frame photographs or images within the collage.

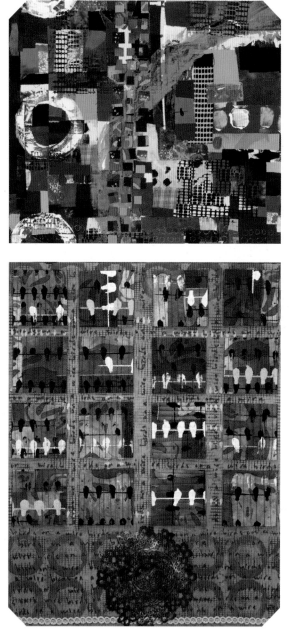

Top: Remnants Collage 17 by Lynn Krawczyk.
Bottom: Blue on a Wire by Lynn Krawczyk.

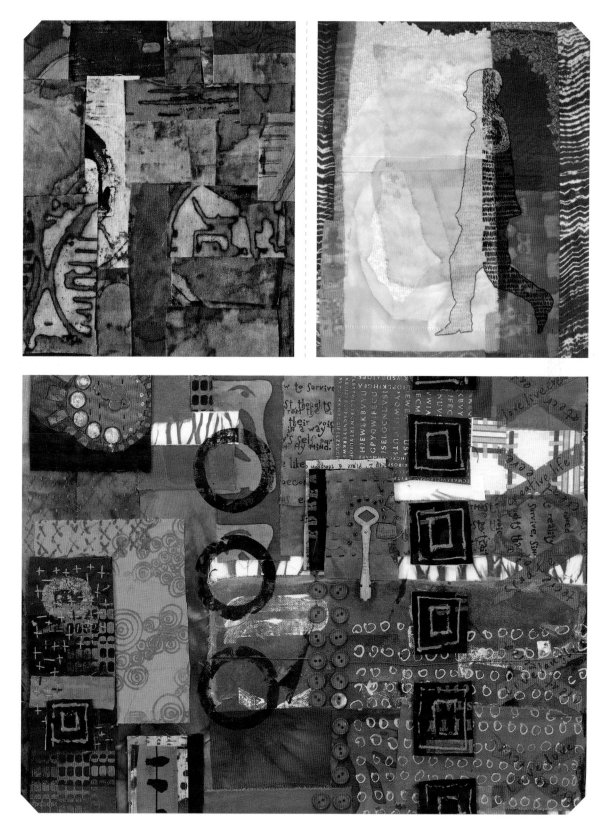

Clockwise from top left: DreamTime Graffiti 1 by Lynn Krawczyk; Transcendental Eclosion by Elizabeth Fram; Remnants Collage 12 by Lynn Krawczyk.

✖ PICTORIAL QUILTS

This type of art quilt is a fabric construction that represents a picture, real or imagined. Pictorial quilts are often scenic, but may also contain people as subjects. This style of quilt is most often hung as artwork, but some pieces may be functional as well.

CHARACTERISTICS

A lot of pictorial quilts are based on a photograph. The artist will either trace the photograph or create a freehand line drawing of it as the initial step in creating the quilt. The drawing is then simplified to remove extraneous details and separated into pieces for the quilt's pattern. The pattern pieces are cut from various fabrics and are appliquéd to a base cloth to create the picture. Free-motion quilting is used to embellish the quilt top and provide shading and details where necessary.

Other pictorial quilts are merely representative of a picture. They are not the literal representation of a photograph, but instead are entirely the work of the artist's imagination.

MATERIALS USED

Appliqué is the primary technique used by pictorial quilt artists. A variety of fabrics are used, with cotton being the most common. Other textiles are used for their different sheens and textures to give dimension and depth to the picture. The fabrics may be hand or machine sewn to the quilt top. Fusible webs, spray adhesives and even glue are sometimes used to adhere the layers before sewing.

Once a pictorial quilt top is complete, the artist often uses machine sewing and free-motion stitching to complete the quilt. Using different colours along with various specialist threads, the quilter is able to create shadows, texture and dimension on their pictorial quilt. Hand embroidery stitching can be used for added details as well.

Letting Go: Gaia Series by Lura Schwarz Smith.

Koi quilt by Sarah Ann Smith.

Top: Spring's Greeting by Frieda Anderson. **Bottom:** Universal Language: Dreams by Lura Schwarz Smith.

ABSTRACT QUILTS

Like abstract art, abstract quilts are unique compositions in which the artist will abandon conventional use of form and colour. Abstract quilts are not meant to resemble a scene, particular pattern or item, but rather an independent work that conveys a representation of the artist's ideas and emotions.

CHARACTERISTICS

Some abstract quilts are designed to be viewed as pieces of artwork, while others are purely functional. The artist often employs traditional piecing and assembling techniques when they are useful and will abandon quilting rules when they do not serve to enhance the piece of art. Some abstract quilts are intentionally designed and then precisely constructed to exact specifications. Other abstract quilt artists approach their fibre art without a specific plan and use improvisational piecing and spontaneity to let their design develop organically.

A wide range of colours is used in abstract quilting. Many quilts make use of starkly contrasting fabrics, while others stick to a more monochromatic palette. Abstract quilters often employ large expanses of negative space and blocks of solid colour in their designs, but they are just as likely to use printed fabrics in large doses with little breathing room between them as well. Shapes and forms may be used repetitively or stand out as a singular motif.

MATERIALS USED

Like most art quilters, abstract quilt artists employ a wide range of textiles. Almost anything goes. Cottons, silks and wools are used together and separately as well as a wide range of textured, dyed and one-of-a kind printed fabrics. Free-motion stitching employs solid, variegated and speciality threads and is used to enhance an artist's design. Other embellishments such as paint, trims, hand stitching and yarn may be included liberally or sparsely in the design of an abstract quilt.

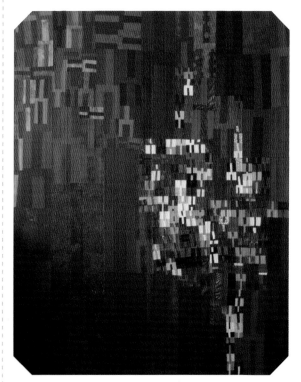

Tuning Fork by Heather Pregger.

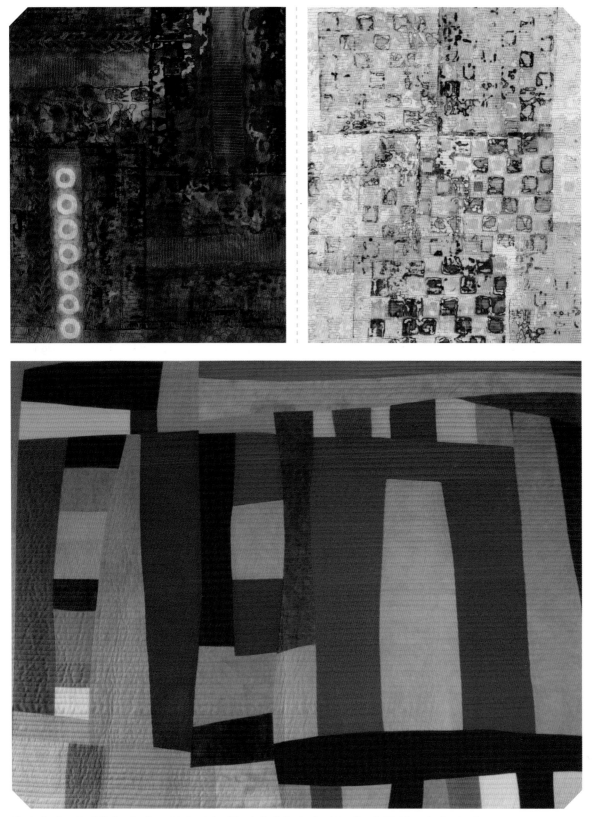

Clockwise from top left: Sunrise Sunset by Carol Ann Waugh; Evolution by Carol Ann Waugh; Big Figure by Heather Pregger.

❖ 10: SASHING AND BORDERS

Sashing and borders are great elements to use when designing your quilts. By framing the individual blocks or the entire quilt top with bands of fabric, you will be able to create more space around your work and highlight the design. From simple strips of fabric to more elaborate pieced bands, there are multiple options to choose from when adding sashing or borders to your quilt.

SEPARATING AND SURROUNDING

Sashing, also known as lattice strips, is made from strips of fabric placed between the quilt blocks to separate them. While sashing surrounds each individual quilt block, borders surround the entire quilt.

SASHING

The sashing can be any width, and may be plain or patchwork. Multiple fabrics can be combined to create framed sashing or to emphasise the blocks' points with cornerstones. Sashing can be used in straight, on-point, horizontal, vertical and alternating quilt settings.

Adding sashing to a quilt will frame the individual blocks, making them stand out and appear separate from their neighbours. By inserting fabric strips between the blocks, you can also add width and length to your quilt top. Sashing creates a break between quilt blocks that will help in squaring up your quilt and camouflaging points that may not match.

Sashing can be an important design element, too. Pick a sashing fabric that will highlight a particular colour in the quilt, or add a new colour to it. Think about how you will quilt the sashing. By using a different quilting design on the sashing than on the remainder of the quilt, you can emphasise the different areas of your work.

BORDERS

Cut from a band of fabric, borders are sewn to all sides of the quilt. The borders can be plain fabric, patchwork pieced or even appliquéd. Their corners may be lapped, mitred or a separate patchwork block. Some quilts, especially medallion settings, may have multiple borders of varying widths.

As with sashing, adding a border to your quilt top will increase its overall size. Make sure that the border's width is appropriate in scale. Borders can match the quilt's background fabric for a minimal, contemporary look. You can also choose to add one in a contrasting or coordinating colour to emphasise your own design. A series of multiple borders in different fabrics or a patchwork border may be the right kind of frame for a simpler quilt design. And don't forget the quilting! Choosing a quilting design that complements your pattern will make for beautiful borders.

Homespun plaid string quilt by Anita Amodeo.

PLAIN SASHING

The simplest form of sashing, plain sashing is made from one fabric. It is sewn to all sides of the quilt block to form a visual break between the blocks. Plain sashing can be any width, but it is important to consider the size of your quilt blocks. In general, smaller blocks benefit from a narrow sashing, whereas larger blocks can accommodate wider strips.

MEASURING, CUTTING AND SEWING

For the sashing between blocks: Determine how wide the finished sashing will be, and add 13 mm (½ in) to accommodate seam allowances. Cut strips of fabric to this width by the length of the unfinished quilt block for the sashing strips. With right sides together and using a 6 mm (¼ in) seam allowance, sew a sashing strip vertically to the quilt block. Press seams towards the quilt block. Sew the blocks with the attached sashing together in rows.

For the sashing between rows: Measure the length of the rows. Cut the sashing to this measurement by the finished width plus 13 mm (½ in). If your rows are long, you may have to sew fabric strips together to reach the required length. With right sides together, sew one length of sashing to each row. Next, sew the rows together to complete the quilt top.

Granny Square quilt by Jessica Fincham.

SASHING TIPS

Sketch it out: There are a couple of different ways to use sashing in your quilt design. You can choose to sash between the blocks and rows, but without sashing on the edges of the quilt, or you could add sashing on all four sides of each block. Each way will yield a different number of sashing strips. It is a good idea to try to sketch out your design before you begin cutting and sewing. This simple step will help you get a good visual grasp of how many sashing strips to cut and where to place them.

Think about grain: When cutting sashing, you can cut either horizontally or vertically from your fabric. The lengthways grain is more stable and is generally preferred for sashing, but the crosswise grain can be used, too. It stretches more easily than the lengthways grain and is a good choice if there is some irregularity to the blocks. If your fabric is a directional print, cut the sashing strips so the pattern reads correctly.

Easy cutting: Using a rotary cutter and ruler is the fastest and easiest way to cut sashing. Cut strips from across the width of fabric and then cut these strips to the sashing size.

TIP
When sewing long strips of sashing to a row, pin them together at the centre and ends, easing the remaining fabric as necessary.

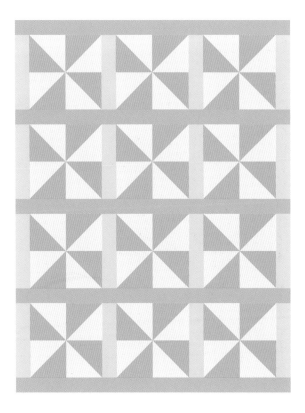

Cut 24 12-cm squares to yield 48 triangles

Cut 24 12-cm squares to yield 48 triangles

Cut 16 21 x 6-cm sashing strips

Cut 5 83 x 6-cm sashing strips

FRAME SASHING

In this method of sashing, two fabrics are used. One fabric is sewn around half the quilt blocks as a frame and the second fabric is sewn similarly around the remaining blocks. The blocks are then laid out, alternating the frame fabrics. Because two neighbouring frames make up the sashing between blocks, the frames should be narrow in width.

Top: Zooey quilt by Lucrecia Hale.
Bottom: Lovely Liberty quilt by Siobhan Rogers.

MEASURING, CUTTING AND SEWING

Cut and sew one frame fabric to half of the quilt blocks. Frame the remaining quilt blocks with the second frame fabric.

Determine the finished frame width and add 13 mm (½ in) to it for seam allowances. Cut two strips of fabric to this width by the length of the unfinished quilt block. Sew one strip to each vertical side of the quilt block using a 6 mm (¼ in) seam allowance.

Measure the block with its vertical frame strips. Cut the horizontal frame strips to this length by the finished width plus 13 mm (½ in). Sew one strip to each the top and bottom of the block.

Lay out the blocks in an alternating pattern and sew them together at the sides to form rows. Once the rows are formed, sew them together to complete the quilt top.

TIP

Draw a diagram of the quilt for a visual reference of how many sashing strips you need.

SASHING WITH CORNERSTONES

Cornerstones are squares of a contrasting fabric that interrupt the sashing where it meets the corners of the quilt blocks.

MEASURING, CUTTING AND SEWING

The sides of the cornerstones are equal in measurement to the width of the sashing strips. Cornerstones made from a single fabric can be cut and sewn to the sashing as individual squares, but strip piecing them will save time.

Begin by cutting the vertical sashing strips to the desired finished width plus 13 mm (½ in) by the length of the quilt block. Sew one strip to the vertical side of each block.

From the sashing fabric, cut a long strip to the length of the unfinished quilt block. From the cornerstone fabric, cut another long strip equal to the unfinished sashing width. Sew these two strips together to create one piece of fabric and press the seam towards the sashing fabric. Using a rotary cutter and ruler, cut the larger pieced fabric into widths of sashing and cornerstone units. Sew these units to the quilt blocks so that the cornerstones interrupt the sashing at the corners. Continue assembly by sewing the blocks into rows and the rows into the quilt top.

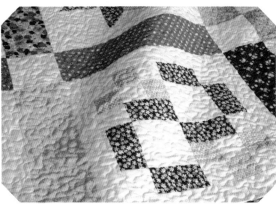

Top: Quilter's Palette quilt by Rita Hodge.
Bottom: Charity quilt and by Amanda Jean Nyberg.

DESIGN IDEA

To give sashing even more character, consider using small patchwork blocks or stars as cornerstones.

✖ PIECED SASHING

Pieced sashing includes multiple fabrics that are sewn together and then used as sashing between quilt blocks. The fabrics can be monochromatic, in graduated colours, or a mish-mash of prints. The pieces in the sashing may be of equal size or pieced from scraps. This type of sashing is best used around very simple quilt blocks or single squares of fabric.

MEASURING, CUTTING AND SEWING

If the pieced sashing will have units that are uniform in size, it's best to start with a sketch. Draw your quilt block and then determine how many pieces you want in the sashing and how big they should be. Make a note of all the finished measurements, add on the appropriate seam allowances and cut the fabrics to size. Once the fabrics are sewn together, sew the sashing to the quilt blocks.

If you are using different-sized scraps, start by sewing the pieces together into a patchwork strip. When the patchwork strip is long enough, use a rotary cutter and ruler to trim it to the required sashing size. Sew the patchwork sashing to the blocks.

With either of these methods, once the sashing is sewn to the blocks, join the blocks into rows. Finally, sew the rows together to complete the quilt top.

Summertime quilt by Amanda Jean Nyberg.

BORDER TIPS

Measure correctly: No matter how consistently the seams are sewn and how precisely the pieces are cut, chances are that your quilt top is not perfectly square. And because there is probably a little bit of irregularity, the measurements for borders are taken through the horizontal and vertical midpoints of the quilt instead of along the sides. First, measure the vertical midpoint for the side borders. Once these borders are attached to the quilt top, measure the horizontal midpoint for the top and bottom borders. When cutting long borders, it's always a good idea to measure twice for a little extra insurance.

Consider grain: Borders cut from the lengthways grain of the fabric are preferable, as they will have considerably less stretch than those cut from the crosswise grain. However, borders pieced from strips of crosswise grain fabric may require less yardage and can be more economical.

Ease the fabric: Many quilters don't pin every seam before it is sewn. When working with borders, though, pins are essential. Start by matching the centre of the border to the centre of the quilt's side and then pinning the two together. Next match and pin both ends. Ease the fabric between the sides and the centres so it lays flat, and pin as you go.

Sewing: When working with long lengths of fabric, use the walking foot so the fabrics feed evenly and easily through your machine. Remove pins as you come to them and press seam allowances towards the borders.

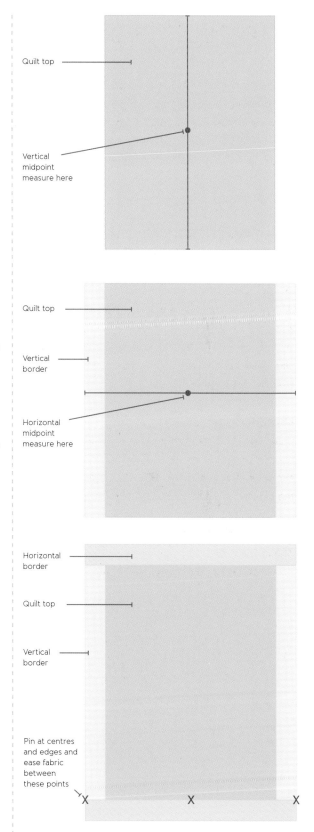

LAPPED BORDERS

The simplest form of a quilt border, the lapped border is easy to sew. Strips of fabric are sewn to the side edges of the quilt top. Top and bottom border strips are then added, overlapping the side borders at the corners.

MEASURING, CUTTING AND SEWING

For a lapped border, begin by measuring the length of the quilt top. Cut two borders to this measurement. Fold each border in half to find its centre and match these marks to the centre of the quilt top's side edges. Match the ends of the borders to the edges of the quilt top and pin in place, easing any excess fabric. Sew the borders to the quilt top and press the seam allowances towards the borders. Next, measure the width of the quilt top including the side borders attached. Cut the top and bottom border strips to this measurement and sew them to the quilt top as you did the side borders.

Top: Bricks and Stones quilt by Rita Hodge.
Bottom: Candy Corn Alternate quilt by Mary Claire Goodwin.

❖ BORDERS WITH INTERRUPTED CORNERS

Borders do not need to be solid pieces of fabric. Using a contrasting fabric or a patchwork block where the borders meet is a traditional design element, known as 'borders with interrupted corners'.

MEASURING, CUTTING AND SEWING

To add borders with interrupted corners, measure the quilt's width and length at the midpoints and cut two strips equal to the length measurement and two strips equal to the width measurement. For the corners, cut four squares, or piece four patchwork blocks, with sides equal in length to the border width.

With the lengthways strips, matching the centres and ends, sew one border to each side of the quilt top. Press the seam allowances towards the borders.

Sew one corner square to each end of the widthwise strips. Press the seams towards the squares. Match the centre of this strip with the centre of the top and bottom edges. At the same time, line up the seams of the corner squares with the side borders' seams. Sew the strips to the quilt top and press the seams towards the top and bottom borders.

Split Rail Fence quilt by Sara Cook.

TIP

Using a walking foot when sewing on borders will ensure that the fabric feeds evenly through the sewing machine.

BORDERS WITH MITRED CORNERS

This type of border meets at the corners with 45-degree angled seams. They are more difficult to sew than lapped or interrupted borders and require extra fabric, but are still very attainable if you take your time.

MEASURING, CUTTING AND SEWING

Measure the quilt's four side lengths by measuring through the midpoints. The only other measurement you need is the border width. To calculate how long to cut the strips, use this formula:

(2 × border width) + length of the quilt side + 114 mm (4½ in) = length of strip

Calculate the strip lengths and cut accordingly. Centre one strip along the side of the quilt and pin it in place. The ends will then overlap the quilt top. Beginning and ending 6 mm (¼ in) from each edge, sew the border in place. Repeat with the remaining three borders, folding any excess fabric out of the way as you go.

Fold the quilt right sides together so that the raw edges of two adjoining borders meet. Line up your ruler with the fold, extending it through the borders. Draw a line along the edge. Pin the borders together and, beginning where your previous stitches end, sew on the line to make the mitre. Unfold the quilt to check your work. If the borders lay flat, trim the seam to 6 mm (¼ in) and press it open. Repeat for the remaining three corners.

Quilt by Erin Burke Harris.

MULTIPLE AND PIECED BORDERS

Adding multiple or pieced borders to your quilt top give you the opportunity to repeat motifs and patterns as well as create added visual interest.

MULTIPLE BORDERS

When framing your quilt with multiple borders, how you add them is dependent on what kind of borders they are. If using lapped or interrupted borders, add one border in its entirety before adding the next one. For mitred borders, join the border strips to each other before sewing them to each side of the quilt as a single unit. Once the borders are attached to the quilt, take care matching the seams when making the mitred corners.

PIECED BORDERS

Seen frequently in traditional patchwork, pieced borders add wonderful repeating designs to a quilt. They are particularly useful for adding more interest to a simple quilt design. However, using repeating blocks takes a little extra planning and calculation to ensure that the borders will fit the quilt top. If the borders are not the right size, you can always add or subtract length to the quilt top or the borders to make them work. Sew pieced borders to a quilt top as lapped or interrupted corner borders.

Busy Little Pinwheel quilt by Amy Sinibaldi.

TIP

For a more contemporary take on pieced borders, use different-sized scraps and improvisational piecing to create a large, patchwork border.

127

◆ 11: EMBELLISHMENT

To make your quilt truly stand out, consider embellishing it in one or more ways.
Traditional, contemporary and art quilts alike can be transformed using special
techniques. Whether you enhance a single design detail or make a more elaborate
series of alterations, embellishing your quilt will give it character and depth.
The use of appliqué, embroidery, paints or trims on your quilt can turn it from
something ordinary into a one-of-a-kind work of art.

◆ APPLIQUÉ

Appliqué is done by taking a cut-out design and sewing it to a background fabric. Most appliqué quilts include different pieces that, when combined, make up a bigger pictorial design.

CHARACTERISTICS

Traditionally sewn by hand, appliqué designs often have pieces that are small in size with curves and points. Modern sewers use both their machines and their hands to add appliqué to a quilt.

TYPES

Needle-turned appliqué is the most traditional form of this art. It's achieved by turning under the seam allowance and raw edges of the appliqué shape as it is hand sewn to the background fabric. To hold the appliqué pieces in place, you can pin them or use a small dab of fabric glue or glue stick.

Reverse appliqué is achieved using two fabrics layered on top of each other. The appliqué shape is cut from the top fabric to reveal a second fabric underneath. The cut edges of the top fabric are turned under, while it is hand sewn to the bottom fabric to reveal the shape.

Machine appliqué is much faster than traditional hand appliqué. The appliqué shapes are cut out and sewn to the background fabric using a zig-zag or satin stitch. The machine's needle should catch both the appliqué fabric and the background fabric as you sew around your design. Leaving the needle in the down position allows you to pivot the fabric around corners and curves continuously. The shape's raw edges can be turned under, but this is not necessary if you use a fusible web to adhere the appliqué fabric to the background fabric before sewing it.

Little Red and Wolfie quilt by Amy Sinibaldi.

APPLICATIONS

Appliqué gives you great flexibility when planning your quilt. It is a wonderful technique to use if your design is elaborate or includes irregular, small or other hard-to-piece shapes. It can be used as the central motif of a medallion quilt with machine-pieced borders or as a small, captivating detail. It can also be repeated, with the same design on a series of smaller blocks. For a modern look, appliqué shapes asymmetrically or haphazardly across the background fabric.

◆ EMBROIDERY

Whether by machine or by hand, over small or large areas, embellishing your quilt with embroidery gives it great character.

CHARACTERISTICS

The technique of embroidery is adding surface designs or ornamentation to fabric using a needle and thread. It is stitched with embroidery thread, perle cotton and thin ribbon, using hand sewing needles in various sizes. A variety of stitches can be used. The most common outline stitches are backstitch, stem stitch and blanket stitch. More elaborate and dimensional stitches are seen in crazy quilting and are also used for embellishment.

REDWORK

Using one colour of thread on white or off-white fabric to embroider the outline of a design is called redwork. Traditionally done with red thread, these days redwork can be embroidered with other colours as long as they contrast with the background fabric.

Top: Marching Raccoon embroidery on baby quilt by Dorie Schwarz.
Bottom: All the Good embroidered quilt by Dorie Schwarz.
Opposite: Bitty Block redwork throw by Leila McCullough.

TYPES

One type of hand embroidery often seen in quilts showcases a particular design on an individual block. The designs in these blocks can be anything from the simplest subject to an very detailed drawing using one or more colours. These blocks are individually embroidered before the quilt top is assembled and then sewn together in a gridded pattern. The blocks may all contain embroidery or they may alternate with pieced or solid blocks in the layout. Sometimes the blocks are sashed with a different fabric to separate and highlight the embroidered works.

Hand embroidery is also used to embellish quilt tops that have already been pieced. The embroidery stitches highlight design elements and give the quilt an extra dimension. Worked through the quilt top and the wadding, this type of hand embroidery is often done freestyle. It may be worked across an entire quilt or just in certain areas.

APPLICATIONS

Embroidery is a great embellishment to contemporary quilts, and there are all kinds of fun and hip embroidery designs available to download. Think about stitching a large medallion as a centrepiece for a quilt, or use embroidery to outline or fill in a portion of a large floral or geometric print. Embroider elaborate stitches along the seams of string-pieced blocks for a modern take on the crazy quilt. Hand stitch a name or date on your quilt top and create a treasured keepsake for yourself or someone you love.

 PAINT

Painting is one of the key items in an art quilter's toolbox. By using paint, you are able to alter fabric to achieve singular, unique results.

CHARACTERISTICS

By applying paint to fabric, you can alter its appearance and feel. Paint can be used to embellish a whole cloth quilt or to add details and depth to a pictorial quilt. Fabric paint comes in a wide range of colours and is specially formulated for use on textiles. Available in liquid and sticks, it can be stencilled, stamped or brushed onto the fabric to achieve various different looks.

TYPES

Acrylic fabric paints are applied to fabric with a brush. They are easy to work with and clean up with soap and water. The option of using different-sized brushes allows the artist to paint small details as well as cover large areas of the quilt. Specially formulated for use on textiles, these fabric paints are smooth, fluid and easy to blend.

Oil-based paint sticks made for textiles are another way to paint as an embellishment. The paint can be applied straight from the stick to the fabric or it can be stencilled on using a short-bristled stencil brush. By placing a textured plate under the fabric, paint sticks can be used like a pencil or crayon to produce a rubbing.

APPLICATIONS

Adding paint significantly changes a fabric's hand and feel. If you paint your project before you quilt it, you will have a completely different look than if you were to paint it after the quilting. Quilting on top of painted fabric will showcase the quilted design, allowing you to see the thread clearly. Of course, having paint on your fabric will make it more difficult to quilt, and your machine needle may also leave visible holes. Painting your quilt after it has been quilted gives a more subtle texture.

It is important to test your paints on the fabric you are using to see what the final effect will be. The paint may appear a different tone when applied to coloured or darker fabrics and will look more textured over dense quilting than smooth fabric. Fabric should be pre-washed before it is painted. If your textile paint requires heat setting, follow the manufacturer's instructions.

Opposite and above: Cherry Sunset quilt with painted fabric by Emma How.

 # TRIMS

Using trims as embellishment adds an instant extra dimension and character to your quilt. Whether in small doses or more liberal amounts, trims allow you to showcase your creativity.

CHARACTERISTICS

Trims are frequently used as embellishments in art quilts, but have some contemporary and traditional applications as well. There is a wide range of trims available to buy. Most of them are flat and woven, allowing you to machine sew them to your quilt top. Some trims, like piping and braid, are more three-dimensional and will require hand stitching or a special sewing machine foot. Trims used in quilts are made from different fibres such as cotton, silk, wool and polyester. Natural-fibre trims may be hand dyed to obtain more colours.

APPLICATIONS

Using trims as embellishments is a great way of showcasing your creativity. If you are making an art quilt, trims can give your project great depth and movement. For a more traditionally inspired quilt, adding ric rac around the edges of small circles can turn a group of simple shapes into a field of flowers. A variety of woven trims with different textures would turn a small quilt into a tactile play mat for a baby.

TYPES

One of the most common trims seen in traditional and contemporary quilting is ric rac. This scalloped, flat trim is available in many different sizes and colours. Frequently seen inset along a quilt's bound edges, ric rac can also be used to frame individual quilt blocks. Its wavy form allows it to lie flat around curves, making it a great choice for bordering appliqué shapes.

Woven ribbons and lace can also be used as embellishments. Due to their linear nature, these trims are best used to create straight lines. They can be sewn across a large expanse of fabric to give the illusion of smaller shapes or quilt blocks. Combined with hand embroidery, they add an extra dimension to crazy quilts.

Other trims such as yarn, piping and braid are most often used on art quilts. They offer the quilter a vast number of embellishment options. However, most of these trims do not lie flat and should therefore be sewn by hand or with a special machine foot fitted.

If your trim is flat, it may be added to the quilt top before quilting. Other, bulkier embellishments should be added once the quilting is complete.

CARRIE STRINE

At first glance, Carrie Strine's quilts appear simple, straightforward and traditional. With a second look, it is obvious that they are much more than this. In her quilts, Carrie successfully marries traditional quilting techniques and patterns with a modern design sensibility. The resulting quilts are stunning works of functional art.

Carrie grew up in central Pennsylvania, surrounded by the art and craft of Amish quilt makers. Raised in a family of makers, she began sewing and designing at a young age. It was while she was pursuing a graduate degree in art that Carrie turned to quilting. She was working on an expansive, hand-cut photo-collage installation when she began to cut fabric for her first quilt. Lacking a sewing machine, Carrie pieced and quilted the entire project by hand. By the time that she was finished, it was obvious to her and those around her that she was hooked.

Although she received a sewing machine from her mother as a graduation gift and uses it for some of her projects, Carrie continues to piece and sew quilts by hand. She finds that she is attracted to long-term, tedious projects, which allow her plenty of time to connect to her work, developing new ideas and stitch patterns as she goes. In a society that is increasingly driven by technology, it is refreshing to see someone committed to time-honoured handcraft and needlework of previous generations.

Carrie's quilts are intricate and well designed with incredible balance of scale, pattern and colour. She combines classic shapes with interesting and decidedly modern colour combinations. The fabrics she uses include contemporary quilting cottons as well as linen, silk, wool and upcycled clothing. The use of these different textiles in a traditional quilt layout provides texture and visual interest – yet another way in which Carrie's quilts are modern interpretations of a traditional craft.

Inspired by contemporary art as well as the tradition of Amish quilting, Carries views her quilts as part of her larger body of artwork. 'Everything I make is part of my art practice', she says. 'That line between a "hobby" (crafting) and my life's work (art) doesn't exist for me.' She is very committed to spending time developing her practice by constantly experimenting with different materials and new techniques, and this is evident in her work.

Double Wedding Ring (in progress).

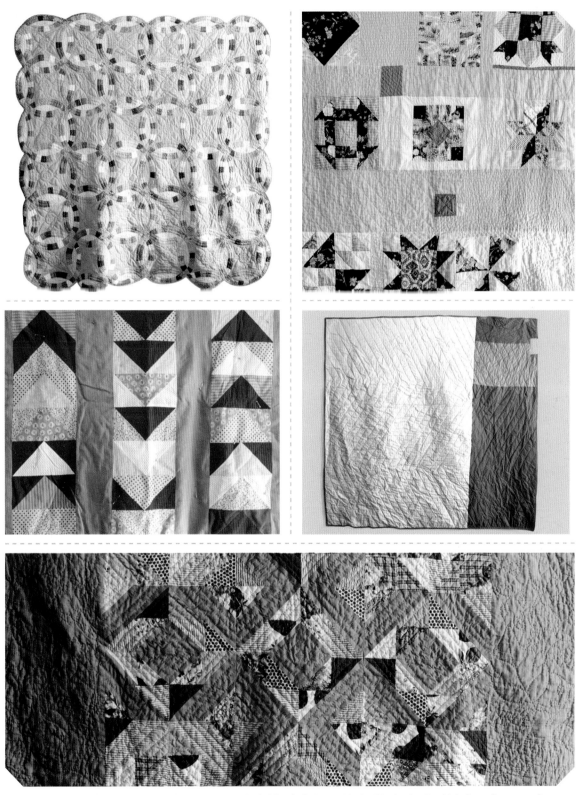

Clockwise from top left: Double Wedding Ring; Eli and Anna's Wedding Quilt; Luxury Moving Blanket; Lattice; Little Goose (in progress).

KAJSA WIKMAN

Kajsa Wikman is a quilt artist who lives and works in the south of Finland. Her cheerful, colourful and whimsical quilts are full of interesting appliqué and free-motion quilting. Her blog, Syko, documents her work and she has also authored a book called Scandinavian Stitches, which contains projects featuring her unique quilting style.

Kajsa has her mother to thank for her love of sewing. When she was a child, Kajsa watched her mother stitch and craft. The two of them took a patchwork class together when Kajsa was 15, and she was immediately enamoured with quilting. She continued sewing as a hobby until she was on maternity leave following the birth of her first child. It was at this point that Kajsa had more time to sew and experiment with fabrics.

While many of Kajsa's pieces are quilts or are quilted, she considers herself an appliqué artist more than a quilter. Her appliqué designs are often inspired by picture books, folk art and her children's artwork. She likes to doodle on paper and then transform those drawings into appliqué with fabric and thread. The black thread that she uses to sew the shapes to fabric and outline them replicates the cartoon-like look of her paper drawings.

Kajsa does employ simple, traditional patchwork piecing in her quilts, but uses is it as more of a background for her imaginative appliqué work than as a feature itself. She uses free-motion quilting to add dimension and character, letting it develop organically as she sews instead of planning it out in advance. Often she will include text, like a song or saying, in the quilting design, as she loves the way handwriting looks. Additionally she finds that mixing traditional elements of fabric and a children's song with an unconventional quilting method gives her quilts a modern edge.

The bright colours of the fabrics that Kajsa uses in her appliquéd motifs contrast well with the neutral tones of the background. She likes to add doses of black and white to her projects, as well. Her overall goal is to give joy through her work. 'Most of my work is both functional and decorative and I love that. But above all, I want my work to be cheerful and happy in a world with so many shades of grey. When people smile at my work, I feel that I have succeeded.'

Clockwise from top: Spring Will Come; Frosty Baby; Once I Caught a Fish.

4

SECTION FOUR
ASSEMBLING

◈ 12: PIECING

There is much more to quilt piecing than simply sewing two fabrics together with a 6 mm (¼ in) seam. Contemporary quilts include piecing methods that range from deliberate sewing by hand to efficient machine piecing and everything in between. Knowing how and when to use these different methods will help you create your own quilts with confidence and ease.

TRADITIONAL PIECING

Traditional piecing is the basic way quilts are put together. It refers to two fabrics being sewn together with a 6 mm (¼ in) seam allowance. This can be achieved by hand or machine sewing. While contemporary quilters may favour the speed and convenience of sewing machines, there are many quilters who prefer the quiet, deliberate art of hand piecing their quilts.

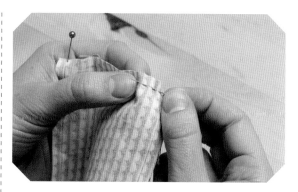

MACHINE PIECING

Machine piecing is the norm in contemporary quilting. It is fast and straightforward with quick results. Sewing straight seams with a machine is easy to do. Curves and Y-seams take a bit more practice, but are still very doable.

Because quilt patterns are often made with precise measurements, it is very important that your seams are accurate. Measure the marked guide on your machine to make sure it is precise. If it is not, place a piece of tape at the correct distance from the needle and use this as your guide when sewing your seams. Many machines have a 6 mm (¼ in) patchwork presser foot, which is extremely helpful when piecing quilts. You simply line up the fabrics' edges with the edge of the foot to sew perfect 6 mm (¼ in) seams.

HAND PIECING

Hand piecing is slower and more labour-intensive than machine piecing. Some quilters enjoy it for its methodical, contemplative and portable nature. It is also a good choice when sewing difficult set-in seams and many small pieces.

In hand piecing, the pieces are cut from fabric and the 6 mm (¼ in) seam allowance is marked on the wrong sides using a pencil. Begin by matching the pieces right sides together along the seam lines. Pin through both fabrics on the seam line and at the corners. Check both sides of your work to make sure the seam lines meet.

Using a single strand of knotted thread, insert the needle on the marked seam line. With a small running stitch (about 1.5 mm/¹⁄₁₆ in), sew along the marked seam line until you get to the other corner. Backstitch a few times, leaving a loop on the last backstitch to pull the thread through. Then press the seam.

✦ FOUNDATION PAPER PIECING

Foundation paper piecing is a way of creating quilt blocks by sewing small pieces of fabric using a paper foundation. The pattern is broken into numbered pieces and the fabrics are sewn in numerical order. When the sewing is complete, the paper is removed from the quilt block. This is a great method for using up scraps.

METHOD 1

In this method the fabric is sewn directly onto the paper. This method is extremely accurate, allowing precise seams and points. Use lightweight, slightly transparent printer or copier paper. Firstly, start by transferring the pattern to the paper. Lay out your fabrics over the shapes to check that each one covers the entire piece where it will be sewn. Then adjust the machine to a shorter stitch length of at least 1.6 to 1.8 mm. This, along with a larger needle (size 90/14 is ideal), will perforate the paper, making it easier to remove. The finished block will be a mirror image of the pattern printed on the paper.

Start with the fabric for piece 1. Place this fabric under the paper so that the fabric's wrong side is facing the paper's wrong side. To avoid the fabric shifting, use a pin to keep it in place. Place the fabric for piece 2 on top of the piece 1, right sides together, and pin. Flip the paper over and sew the line between pieces 1 and 2. Now fold the paper back along the sewn line to expose the seam. Using a small ruler and a rotary cutter, trim the seam allowance to 6 mm (¼ in). Flip the paper over to the fabric side and press using your fingers or a dry iron. Continue adding pieces in this manner, following their numeric order. Trim the block to the pattern's outer edge and press.

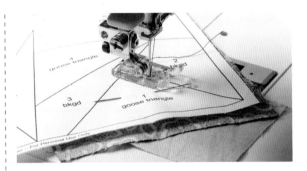

METHOD 2

This method uses greaseproof paper as its foundation. Transfer the design to the dull side of the paper. Carefully cut the design apart and iron each piece to the right side of the appropriate fabric. Using a rotary cutter and ruler, trim the fabric 6 mm (¼ in) from the templates' edges for a seam allowance.

Remove the greaseproof paper from pieces 1 and 2 and sew them together with a 6 mm (¼ in) seam. Press the seam, then continue adding pieces one at a time, in numerical order. When all the seams have been sewn, press the finished block.

✦ ENGLISH PAPER PIECING

English paper piecing stabilises the fabric with a paper template to ensure accuracy. The fabric is hand tacked to the template, folding the seam allowance under as it is stitched. Once all the pieces are tacked, they are sewn to each other along the shape's folded edge.

The paper templates are made from lightweight card, available to buy in different shapes and sizes. You can also make your own templates or download and print free ones. The paper is not removed until the entire block is pieced, so you will need one template for each piece you are sewing.

METHOD
Place the template on a piece of fabric and secure it using a pin or a small dab from an acid-free glue stick. Cut the fabric around the template, leaving a 6 mm (¼ in) seam allowance. Fold the seam allowance towards the back of the shape and tack in place by sewing through the fabric and paper. When you reach a corner, overlap the seam allowances so the fabric is folded neatly along the template's edges.

To join two shapes, hold the tacked pieces right sides together, matching edges. With a single strand of knotted thread and using a small whipstitch, sew the sides together along the fold. Be careful not to sew through the paper. Backstitch a couple of times at the corner, leaving a loop to pull the thread through. When you unfold the seam, the stitches should not show on the right side of your work. Once all of the edges are sewn on a piece, remove the tacking stitches and the paper template and press.

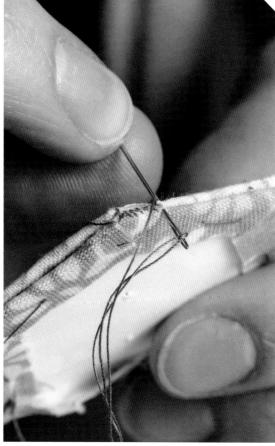

TIP

To make cutting multiple shapes faster, stack up to four pieces of fabric and use your rotary cutter and ruler to cut around the template with a 6 mm (¼ in) seam allowance.

◆ CHAIN PIECING

Chain piecing is a fast, effective way to sew pieces together assembly line-style. It is ideal for when your pattern calls for multiples of the same block or you have many pieces to sew in one sitting.

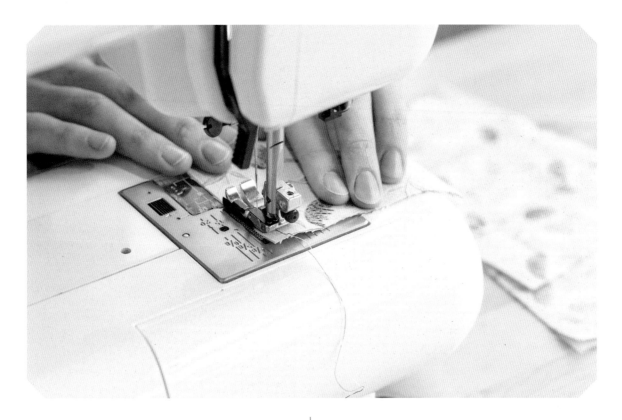

METHOD

Begin by matching up your pieces into pairs. Align them right sides together along the sewing edge. Place these units next to your sewing machine with the edge you are sewing facing to the right.

Raise the presser foot and place the first unit under it. Line up the edges with the 6 mm (¼ in) marking on your machine, lower the presser foot and sew the pieces together. When you reach the end of the pieces, do not cut your thread and leave the presser foot down. Sew a few more stitches and then feed the next unit under the presser foot to sew the seam.

Continue in this manner until all the pairs are sewn. Once you have completed your piecing, clip the threads between each unit. They are now ready for pressing.

TIP
Use the 6 mm (¼ in) piecing foot for your machine if you have one.

✧ STRIP PIECING

Strip piecing is great when a quilt pattern requires a series of squares or rectangles in a particular colour order. Instead of cutting and sewing individual squares one to one, long strips of fabric are sewn together and then cut into smaller units. This method significantly lessens sewing and cutting time and is more accurate than traditional piecing.

METHOD
Begin by cutting strips of the desired height from the width of the fabric. Make sure you remember to include seam allowances. Lay the strips out in the order that they need to be pieced together. With right sides together, sew the first strip to the second strip using a 6 mm (¼ in) seam allowance. Maintaining the correct seam allowance is crucial to ensure your pieces are of uniform size. If at any time you notice that your seam allowance is becoming smaller or

larger, stop, rip out your stitches and begin again. Sew the second strip to the third strip as explained above. Continue in this manner until all strips are sewn together. Press all the seams in one direction.

To cut the pieced strips into smaller units, lay the fabric right side down on the cutting mat. Line up your ruler to the appropriate measurement and then cut with a rotary cutter.

Strip piecing is best done without pinning, which may cause slight puckers or stretching. It is advisable, however, to mark the centre point of each strip with a pin or small crease and then to match these marks to ensure that the strips will be evenly pieced. If you are sewing more than two or three strips together, try to alternate the direction in which they are sewn. By doing so, you will eliminate the slight curve or bend that can occur when sewing many strips in the same direction. Finally, don't piece strips that are longer than the customary width of fabric. The longer your strips are, the more likely you are to encounter stretching or inaccurate seams.

TIP
Using jelly rolls when strip piecing is a great time-saver. With the strips already cut to the same width and length, all you have to do is sew them together and cut them into strips.

✦ STRING PIECING

String piecing is a form of scrap quilting in which long thin strips of fabric of varying widths, or 'strings', are sewn together to create blocks. Strings are often not cut with the grain and are too thin to yield other shapes. Because most string piecing is done using a foundation, these small widths and off-grain pieces are stabilised and can be used to create a one-of-a-kind quilt.

TYPES

While string piecing is frequently done on square foundations, other shapes create stunning results as well. Stacked string rectangles can create interesting stripes and coin-style quilts. Creatively pieced triangles can be combined to create stars and spiders' webs. Many square string-pieced quilt blocks have a centre string that is consistent in size and colour throughout the quilt top. When the blocks are sewn together, these centre strips match to create a striped or 'X' pattern. Because string-pieced quilts are made mostly from scraps, the other strips won't necessarily match up at the seams, and the seams aren't always straight. These inconsistencies are what give string quilts their charm and character.

FOUNDATION

Generally, the foundation for string piecing is muslin (or another lightweight fabric) or paper. Fabric foundations get incorporated into your quilt top, whereas paper foundations are removed when your block is complete. Reduce the stitch length to 1.6 to 1.8 mm when piecing on paper foundations. This will almost perforate the paper, allowing you to tear it off easily.

Above: Summer string pieced quilt by Sara Cook.

METHOD 1

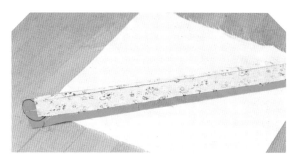

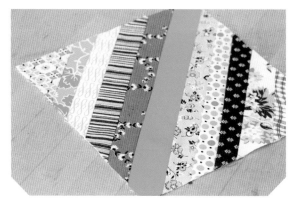

METHOD 2

Sewing and then flipping is the most common method for piecing strings. The first string is placed diagonally across the centre of the foundation square, right side up. The second string is placed on top of the first one, right side down, and sewn using a 6 mm (¼ in) seam allowance. Once sewn, it is flipped over and pressed. Continuing in this manner, additional strings are added until the entire foundation is covered.

Another way is to simply sew the strips together without a foundation. This is a great option if you want all of your shapes to be string-pieced with the same fabrics. To do this, line your fabrics up and sew the different strings together with a 6 mm (¼ in) seam allowance. Press. Then, using a template, cut shapes from the string-pieced fabric.

◈ GRID PIECING

Grid piecing is a fast and effective way to create half-square triangles. The time spent cutting and sewing is dramatically reduced and, due to the way these blocks are pieced, there is no stretching along the triangles' bias edges.

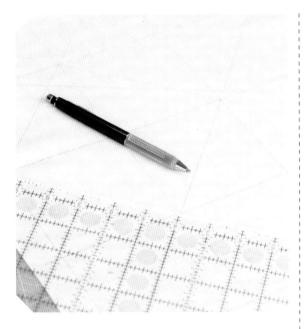

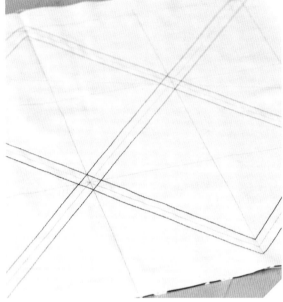

METHOD

To create the grid, take the finished block's measurements and add 2.5 cm (1 in) to it to account for seam allowances. This will be the size of the squares in the grid. Each square will produce two half-triangle blocks. Count how many blocks from the same two fabrics you need and divide that number by two. If your pattern requires an odd number of blocks, round this number up to the next whole number. You will have one extra block when you are finished.

The amount of fabric you need will depend on the size of the entire grid. If you need 24 finished blocks at 7.5 cm (3 in) each, you will be sewing 12 squares at 10 cm (4 in) each, laid out in a 3 × 4 grid.

The measurement of the entire grid will be 30 × 41 cm (12 × 16 in). Cut your fabric slightly bigger than these measurements to ensure you have enough.

Lay your fabrics right sides together with the lighter-coloured fabric on top. Using a water-soluble pen or pencil and a ruler, mark the grid on the fabric. Once the squares are marked, take the pen and ruler and mark through them on the diagonal. If you don't want to draw directly on the fabric, mark the grid on a piece of paper and then pin this onto your fabrics. Pre-printed grid papers are available to buy, but they only come in certain sizes.

To piece the triangles, sew 6 mm (¼ in) on each side of the diagonal lines. If you have a 6 mm (¼ in) presser foot for your machine, first line up its edge with the marked lines, and sew. If you don't, mark additional lines 6 mm (¼ in) to each side of the diagonal lines and stitch along these.

When you have finished sewing, cut the blocks apart. Using a rotary cutter and ruler, cut along all marked lines to separate the squares. Unfold the blocks and press the seam towards the lighter-coloured fabric. The blocks will be slightly larger than the finished measurement. With a rotary cutter and ruler, trim them to the correct size.

✦ IMPROVISATIONAL PIECING

Improvisational piecing is a technique used frequently by contemporary quilters. It is piecing freeform, without measuring or precise cutting. There is no worrying about perfectly straight seams and matching points and, as a result, the quilt often has slightly curved or wonky lines. For many quilters, it is a great creative exercise in letting go of the constraints of traditional piecing. By making design decisions in the moment with what you have in front of you, there is no over-thinking or excessive analysing. This approach to piecing quilts results in visually interesting and entirely unique designs.

HOW TO DO IT

Improvisational piecing works best when using fabrics of different lengths and widths. Because small pieces of fabric are often used, your scrap bin is a great place to start. You can sew many small pieces of fabric together to create a longer length when necessary.

To start piecing, take two pieces of fabric and sew them together using a 6 mm (¼ in) seam allowance. Press the seam to one side. Choose a third piece of fabric and decide how you want to add it to the fabrics you have already sewn. You may have to use a rotary cutter and ruler to trim uneven edges, but otherwise no squaring is necessary. Sew the third piece to the first two and continue adding fabrics until you are satisfied with the look.

THINGS TO KEEP IN MIND

When improvisational piecing, there really are no rules. That doesn't mean that you should approach improvisational piecing without following some guidelines, though. Placing constraints on your work may lead to a more cohesive project. For example, you might consider using a limited colour palette or dividing your fabrics into light and dark values to give the quilt contrast and interest. Using many solids and limited prints, or vice versa, could provide another set of parameters for your project. You could also improvisational piece a particular pattern, such as log cabins or stars, by cutting the pieces without rulers or templates for a looser look. Don't forget to think about negative space and how it might add to or detract from your overall design.

TIP

Improvisational piecing is meant to be liberating and fun. Don't worry about making mistakes. The more you do it, the easier it gets.

◆ PIECING WADDING

The more you quilt, the more scraps you will accumulate. Not just fabric scraps, either. Leftover bits of wadding can be pieced together to make a larger piece. This is both economical and easy to do.

WHEN TO PIECE WADDING

Piecing wadding is great for quilts that will be machine or hand quilted, because the quilting stitches will further stabilise the wadding. If you plan on tying your quilt, it is better to use a single piece of wadding. Quilts that are tied do not have enough stitches to ensure that a pieced wadding will stay adequately sewn together.

All types of wadding can be pieced, but it is important to make sure that you are piecing similar scraps together. Do not mix fibre content or lofts in order to avoid bulky seams or problems when the quilt is laundered. Low-loft waddings are great candidates for machine piecing. Mid- to high-loft waddings are best pieced by hand. In any scenario, use a thread that matches the colour of the wadding scraps so that it will not show through your quilt top.

TIP
Fusible interfacing (shown above) is sold on a roll and allows you to easily fuse leftover wadding pieces together. The thin material doesn't add bulk, as overlapping the layers would, or stiffness, and saves you the time that joining wadding by sewing takes.

MACHINE METHOD

HAND METHOD

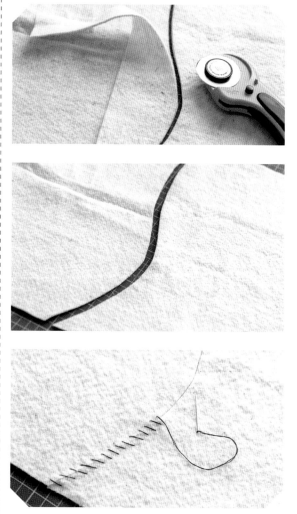

If the scraps don't have straight edges, trim them so that the two pieces butt up against each other. Once the edges are straight, you are ready to sew. Place the pieces under the presser foot so they meet in the centre, but do not overlap. Using a wide zig-zag stitch, sew the wadding pieces together. Take care not to stretch the wadding to avoid creating ridges at the seam line.

Lay the wadding scraps on a large, flat surface, overlapping them by a few centimetres. With scissors or a rotary cutter, cut a slight wavy line through both waddings where they overlap. Remove the small wadding remnants from above and below the wadding. The two wavy edges should align perfectly. Using a single strand of knotted thread, whip stitch the wadding pieces together without stretching or pulling the wadding. The wavy line should help eliminate any ridges or folds in the wadding that may be created if the hand stitches do not hold over time.

◆ PIECING BACKING FABRICS

Traditionally, pieced quilt backs are made from one fabric, with either horizontal or vertical seams. In contemporary quilts, it is common to see backs sewn from more than one fabric and, often, with patchwork strips or extra quilt blocks incorporated as design elements.

METHOD

In order to make the quilt back large enough, it will most likely need to be pieced from multiple widths of standard 107 cm (42 in)-wide fabric. Quilt backing fabrics up to widths of 305 cm (120 in) are available – however, they do not come in a large range of colours and may be hard to find.

Measure the quilt top as a reference for how big the backing should be. It's a good idea to sketch this out on a piece of paper, noting the width and length measurements. The quilt back should be 7.5–10 cm (3–4 in) larger than the quilt top on all sides. Add 15–20 cm (6–8 in) to your quilt top measurements to find the size of the backing.

Using your sketch for reference, decide how you want to piece the backing. You can choose one fabric or a combination of different fabrics. Adding a strip in a contrasting colour or patchwork between larger pieces of fabric is a good way to make the seams look more intentional. It's also a nice added design element and a good use of extra quilt blocks or scraps from the quilt top.

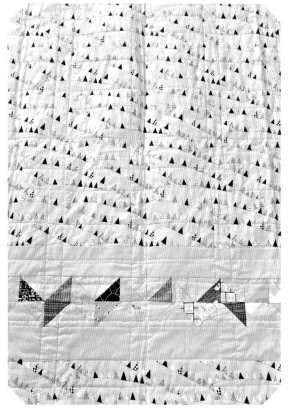

When the design of the backing is complete, indicate the different pieces on your sketch and calculate how big they will need to be cut. Be sure to include 13 mm (½ in) for each seam allowance. Remove selvedges from the backing fabric and then measure it to get its exact width. Trimming these bound edges will help stop puckering and ensure that the backing lies flat. Cut the fabric(s) to the measurements on your sketch and then sew them together with a 13 mm (½ in) seam allowance. Press all seams open. Using a larger seam allowance stabilises the seams, and pressing them open reduces the bulk and makes quilting across them easier.

Opposite: Quilt by Erin Burke Harris.
Above left: Back of Zooey quilt by Lucrecia Hale.
Above right: Pow Wow quilt by Melissa Robinson.

TIP
Take care when using directional fabrics in your backings. Make sure that you use them with vertical seams so that the fabric reads correctly.

◈ 13: QUILT SANDWICHING

Assembling the quilt top, wadding and backing is commonly called quilt sandwiching. With information on how to choose the right wadding for your project as well as how to prepare the sandwich for quilting, this chapter will help you get one step closer to transforming fabric and thread into a finished quilt.

✧ TYPES OF WADDING

Wadding is the inner layer of a quilt that gives it dimension and its warming properties. Knowing a bit about the different fibres and thicknesses of commercially available waddings will make choosing the right one for your project easy.

LOFT

'Loft' refers to the thickness of a wadding. As a rule, the higher the loft, the warmer the quilt. Low-loft waddings are generally less than 6 mm (¼ in) thick and are good choices for both machine and hand quilting. They will give the quilt a traditional look with little dimension and lightweight warmth. Medium-loft waddings range between 6 mm (¼ in) and 13 mm (½ in) in thickness. With more dimension and warmth than low-loft waddings, they are easily quilted by hand or machine. High-loft waddings are over 13 mm (½ in) thick and are mostly made from polyester. These waddings are most suited to tying and will result in a puffy-looking quilt.

FIBRES

Cotton: 100 per cent cotton waddings are soft and stable. Generally available in low loft, they are suitable for machine and hand quilting. They are machine washable, but can shrink up to 5 per cent. Cotton waddings are a great choice for a traditional, crinkly look and provide good, breathable warmth.

Polyester: Polyester waddings are usually lightweight, durable and stable. They are available in various thicknesses and work well for machine and hand quilting. High-loft polyester waddings are especially good for tying quilts. Because they are made from a synthetic fibre, polyester waddings do not breathe and are flammable. They are machine washable and do not shrink.

Cotton/Poly blends: Combining the softness of cotton with the stability of polyester, cotton/poly blended waddings work well for hand and machine quilting. They are readily available in low to medium lofts and are machine washable. Shrinkage is common, but is not as great as with a 100 per cent cotton wadding. Some cotton/poly blended waddings can be pre-washed to avoid shrinkage.

Wool: Wool wadding is very warm but not as stable as other waddings and the loft may vary; however, it is still a good choice for machine and hand quilting. It may be washable, but do follow the manufacturer's directions to avoid felting or clumping. Quilts with wool wadding tend to be soft and drapeable.

Bamboo: Sustainable and eco-friendly, bamboo waddings are very strong but still soft with low loft. They are machine washable with very little shrinkage, and provide nice drape in both hand and machine quilted quilts.

◈ MAKING THE QUILT SANDWICH

Once you have your quilt top sewn, your backing ready and the wadding chosen, it's time to make your quilt sandwich. Taking the time to properly sandwich and tack your quilt will ensure that it does not shift, bunch or pucker.

You'll need a large, flat surface to work on. Most often, this is the floor. If you lack the floor space to spread out your quilt, local quilt stores will often let customers use their workspace for sandwiching. Alternatively, if you are making a smaller quilt or project, your dining table may well be big enough. Either way, make sure there is plenty of space on all sides of the quilt so you can move around it easily.

1 SECURE YOUR FABRIC

A. You will need tape to temporarily adhere the fabric to the work surface. Painter's tape is preferable, as it is low-tack and will not damage the quilt or the floor, but masking tape also works and is a good second choice. If you are working on a table, binder clips are great for clamping the fabric to the tabletop.

B. Begin by laying the quilt back on the floor with its right side down. Secure the centre of the top edge to the floor using a piece of tape. Gently smooth out any wrinkles and puckers along the top edge and secure the top corners to the floor using tape. Continue smoothing out the back, from the top down, keeping it taut without stretching it. Tape the remaining corners and edges as you go.

TIP
Remember that the quilt back and wadding should be 7.5 cm (3 in) to 10 cm (4 in) larger than the quilt top on all sides.

2 ADD THE WADDING

Once the quilt backing is taped down, it's time to add the next layer: the wadding. Spread the wadding down on top of the quilt back and smooth out any wrinkles or creases. Be careful not to tug on it or stretch it, as some waddings are easily torn when over-handled. If you plan on spray tacking your quilt, stop here and follow the directions for spray tacking (see page 167). For pin and hand tacking, continue here.

3 POSITION THE QUILT TOP

Centre the quilt top, right side up, on top of the wadding. Just as you did with the other layers of the quilt sandwich, smooth the quilt top out so it is flat and free of wrinkles. Wadding tends to grip the fabric firmly so you may have to lift the quilt top up if you need to reposition it. As soon as the quilt top is in place, you are ready to tack the quilt.

 # TACKING

Tacking is the temporary method that holds all three layers of the quilt sandwich together as you sew them together with quilting stitches. There are three popular tacking methods to consider.

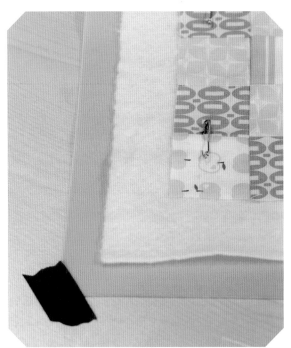

HAND TACKING

Hand tacking is a technique in which large, hand-sewn stitches hold the quilt sandwich together. It is used most frequently with hand quilting. Choose thread in a colour that contrasts with the quilt top so the tacking stitches are easy to see. Thread a long, thin needle with the end of a spool of thread. Starting in the centre of the quilt and working your way to the edges, make 2.5–3 cm (1–1.5 in) stitches through all layers of the quilt sandwich in a grid pattern. Tack in horizontal, vertical, and diagonal lines, ensuring that the tacking stitches are no farther than 10 cm (4 in) apart. Remove the tacking stitches after you finish hand quilting by clipping the threads and pulling them from the quilt.

PIN TACKING

Pin tacking is a good method for machine quilting. Use rustproof curved safety pins made especially for quilting. The curve makes it easy to bring the pin point up through all three layers of the quilt sandwich. To pin tack, begin in the centre of the quilt top, working toward the edges and corners. Place the pins about 10–15 cm (4–6 in) apart in a staggered grid, or brick-like layout. When quilting, remove the pins as you come to them to avoid breaking your needle. Leaving the pins open when you store them will save time when you tack your next quilt.

TIP
Always spray the wadding, never the fabric.

SPRAY TACKING

Spray tacking is done using a temporary adhesive spray to keep all the layers of the quilt sandwich together. Unlike hand and pin tacking, spray tacking is done as the quilt sandwich is made instead of when it is complete. Choose a spray that is made for use with fabric, sticks well, is repositionable and will wash out. It's always a good idea to test the adhesive on scraps before using it on your quilt.

To spray tack, lay the backing on the floor, smooth out the wrinkles and tape it down. Place the wadding on top of the backing so it is flat and without creases, then gently fold back the wadding to its centre. Lightly spray the wadding with the adhesive, and carefully smooth it back over the quilt backing. Once you have finished one half, repeat with the second half of the wadding. To add the quilt top, centre it on top of the wadding so it is flat and smooth. Fold the quilt top along its centre and spray the exposed wadding with the spray adhesive. Lay the quilt top back on the sprayed wadding and smooth it out from the centre to the edges. Repeat this process with the second half of the quilt top.

◈ TRANSFERRING THE QUILTING DESIGN

When it comes time to quilt your quilt, you need to decide what kind of design you will use. Outline quilting, stitching in the ditch and some free-motion quilting are easy to manage without marking your quilt top, but other quilting designs will need to be transferred to the fabric before you can sew.

There are two main ways to transfer the design to your quilt top: tracing and stencilling. Tracing the pattern is a good option for light- to medium-coloured fabrics. To do this, you will need access to a lightbox or a large, sunny window. A paper with the design is taped down on the lightbox and the quilt top is placed on top of the design. It's a good idea to tape the quilt top down as well in order to keep it taut and to keep it from shifting. Turn the lightbox on and trace the design onto the fabric with the marking tool of your choice. Once the design has been completely transferred, you can make the quilt sandwich.

Stencilling the design onto the quilt top is helpful when you have darker fabrics, but works just as well on lighter colours, too. You will find a large variety of pre-made plastic stencils at the quilt store or you can make your own using template plastic or lightweight card. Lay the stencil on your quilt top and use a bit of masking tape to keep it in place. Using your preferred marking tool, transfer the design to the quilt top.

MARKING TOOLS

Different marking tools all have advantages and disadvantages. With a little trial and error, you'll find one that works well for your project. It's always wise to test your marking tools on scrap fabric first.

▶ **Water-soluble markers** – Available in blue and white, their marks are easily removed with water, but become permanent when exposed to heat or an iron.

▶ **Chalk pencils** – Good for marking, but marks rub away easily.

▶ **Quilter's pounce** – A plastic box with fabric on one side is filled with chalk that is 'wiped' over stencils to transfer the quilting design. It's very efficient at transferring large designs, but can rub off.

▶ **Wax-free transfer paper** – Transfer paper is placed between the design and the quilt top. The design is traced with a pencil, leaving a transfer on the quilt top. It's easily washed or rubbed off.

✦ 14: QUILTING METHODS

Sewing the quilting stitches is the penultimate step on your journey to a finished quilt. Hand quilting, tying and various forms of machine quilting all have their place in a contemporary quilter's arsenal of techniques. Understanding the mechanics of these different quilting methods will give you the confidence to choose the perfect way to quilt your projects.

◈ HAND QUILTING

Hand quilting is characterised by small, hand-sewn running stitches that are evenly sized and spaced on the front and the back of the quilt.

WHAT YOU NEED

Quilt frame or hoop – This will keep the quilt layers together and the fabric taut. Quilt frames come in various different sizes and styles, ranging from smaller, portable, lap-sized models to larger, free-standing versions.

Hand quilting needles, called betweens – These are shorter than traditional hand sewing needles, and are good for making small stitches.

Thimble – This is essential to push the needle through the quilt's layers.

Thread – Hand quilting thread is strong and durable. It is coated with beeswax to slide through the fabric easily and prevent any twisting or tangling. Perle cotton is another option favoured by contemporary quilters. It is much thicker than thread and the resulting stitches sit up on the fabric, making them more visible.

METHOD

1. Begin by knotting a length of thread no longer than 45 cm (18 in). Place your needle into the quilt about 13 mm (½ in) from where you want the first stitch to begin. Do not push the needle through all the layers to the back. Instead, bring the tip of the needle out of the top fabric at the starting point. Tug very gently on the thread to pop the knot under the fabric. The knot will catch in the wadding and will not be visible from the front or the back.

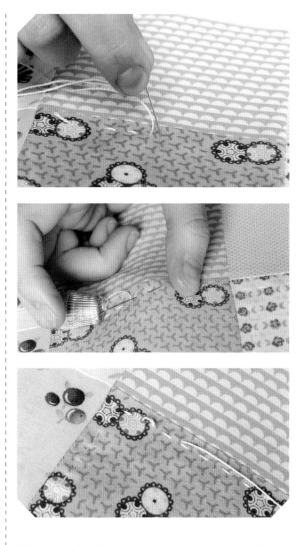

2. To make the first stitch, insert the needle vertically into the fabric. Use your non-sewing hand to feel the tip of the needle on the back of the quilt, but do not pull it all the way through. Slightly rock the needle to pick up a new stitch, and bring the tip back up to the top of the quilt. Return the needle to its vertical position and repeat to make another stitch. Once you have a few stitches on the needle, pull the thread through. When it is time to change threads or end your quilting, always stop with one stitch left. Knot the thread and make your final stitch. Pop the knot under the fabric into the wadding like you did in the beginning and then cut the thread.

◈ TYING A QUILT

Tying a quilt is a simple and effective way to sew the layers of the quilt sandwich together.

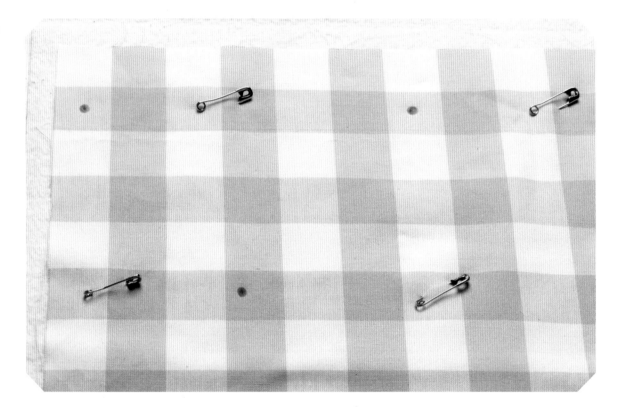

WHAT YOU NEED

► **Thread or yarn** – You can tie a quilt with almost any kind of thread or yarn. Embroidery thread, perle cotton, crochet thread and woollen yarn are all good choices.

► **Needle** – Choose a sharp needle with an eye big enough to accommodate the thread you are using. A curved needle may be helpful.

► **Ruler and marking tool** – A large quilter's ruler is helpful when aligning and marking the spots where the quilt will be tied.

METHOD

Lay the tacked quilt down on a large, flat surface. A table or the floor work well. If you find the quilt is moving a lot, use masking tape to keep it in place. Next, mark the spots where you want the ties to be located using a pencil or other marking tool. The spots should be equal in distance from each other and are often marked in a grid formation. The wadding you choose will determine the maximum distance you can leave between the ties. Make sure to check the package to see what the manufacturer recommends for the wadding you are using.

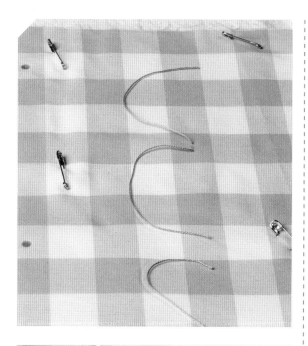

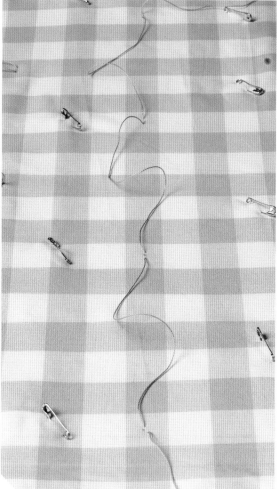

Without cutting or knotting, thread your needle with a single strand of yarn or thread. Starting at the centre of the left side of the quilt, insert the needle just to the left of the first marked spot. Make sure that the needle goes through all three layers and bring it up just to the other side of the mark. Leaving some slack in the thread, continue on to the next marked spot and sew it as you did the first. Keep sewing across the entire row until you have completed a stitch at each of the marks. Cut the thread, leaving a tail that is at least 5 cm (2 in) long.

Continue stitching across the rows of marked spots until they are all sewn. To finish the ties, cut the thread between each marked spot to create long tails. Use a triple knot to tightly secure each tie (right over left, left over right, and right over left). Then carefully trim the ends to 13 mm (½ in) or the desired length.

◈ MACHINE QUILTING WITH A WALKING FOOT

Machine quilting using a walking foot is a good option for machine-sewn, straight quilting lines using a home sewing machine.

WHAT YOU NEED

▶ **Walking foot** – This special presser foot allows you to sew through multiple layers without the fabric shifting or puckering. Unlike a regular presser foot that holds the fabric in place while the feed dogs pull it through the machine, a walking foot has a set of teeth that pull the top layer of fabric at the same rate as the feed dogs pull the bottom layer. It attaches to the presser foot shaft and has an extension arm that is placed over the needle clamp. This extension arm is what signals the walking foot to move at the same pace as the feed dogs. Walking feet are available for most sewing machines. Some of them come with guides that make quilting evenly spaced lines easy. If your machine did not come with one, take your manual to the sewing store to ensure you buy the correct walking foot for your model.

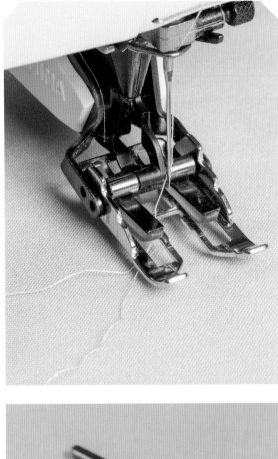

▶ **Machine quilting needle** – Quilting needles have a slim shaft and a fine, slightly rounded point and are made for use when quilting with a home sewing machine. Microtex needles are also a good option. Their sharp points easily sew through layers of the quilt sandwich. Thicker, speciality threads may require a topstitch needle, which has a larger eye.

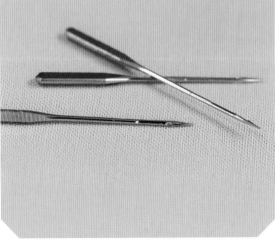

HOW TO DO IT

Insert your quilt under the walking foot where
you want to begin. Lower the walking foot and sew
one stitch. Raise the walking foot and pull the top
thread tail to bring the bobbin thread tail up to the
surface of the quilt. Lower the presser foot, hold the
thread tails to the side and sew two or three stitches.
Backstitch over the stitches you just sewed and then
begin quilting. Follow your marked lines or use a
guide until you have reached the end. Finish your
quilting by backstitching to ensure the stitches do
not come loose.

TIP

If you have pin tacked your quilt, stop sewing
and remove the pins as you come to them so they
do not interfere with the walking foot.

◆ FREE-MOTION MACHINE QUILTING

Free-motion machine quilting is a technique that allows the quilter to stitch in all directions, achieving curves, swirls and other non-linear designs.

WHAT YOU NEED

▶ **Darning/Free-motion foot** – This specialist presser foot has either a circle or open toe at the base that is made of metal or clear plastic.

▶ **Machine quilting needle** – Because free-motion quilting puts stress on the needle, it is important to choose a strong one and to change it frequently. A size 90/14 machine quilting, universal or Microtex needle is a good choice.

▶ **Quilting gloves** – It may be helpful to wear gloves that have rubberised fingertips as they will give you a better grip on the fabric as it moves.

HOW TO DO IT

Begin by lowering the feed dogs and setting the stitch length to 0. Place your quilt sandwich under the darning foot at the place where you want to begin. Lower the presser foot and take one stitch. Gently pull the top thread tail to bring the bobbin thread to the top of the quilt. Holding the thread tails to the side, stitch a few times in the same spot to anchor the thread. Using your hands to help guide the quilt sandwich, begin moving it according to the pattern you are using. After sewing for 2.5 cm (1 in), stop with the needle in the down position. Carefully clip the thread tails close to the top and then continue to quilt. To finish quilting, take a few stitches in one spot to knot the thread. Cut the top thread close to the quilt top and the bobbin thread close to the quilt back.

THINGS TO KEEP IN MIND

Practise, practise, practise. Free-motion quilting may be difficult at first, but the more you do it, the easier it becomes.

The rate at which you move your hands controls the length of the stitches. Moving the quilt slowly results in small stitches. Long stitches come from moving the quilt faster. Finding the right rhythm takes time. At first it's a good idea to quilt several small quilt sandwiches made from scraps to get the feel for how much pressure you need on the foot pedal in relation to how fast you move the quilt.

Check the tension on the front and back of the quilt and make adjustments if necessary. Using the same coloured thread in the bobbin and the needle as well as using a patterned fabric for the quilt back will help hide any irregularities in the quilting.

Jubilee Vintage Triangles quilt by Sara Cook.

✧ LONG-ARM QUILTING

Long-arm quilting is the process in which the quilt top, wadding and back are attached to a large frame and sewn together using an industrial-strength machine.

Long-arm quilting machines are guided either by hand or by computer. The hand-guided machines have two handles and are moved just as you would draw on paper. In this case, however, the needle is the 'pencil' and the quilt is the 'paper'. Quilting designs can be sewn using a template, called a pantograph, or sewn freehand. Computer-guided machines are pre-programmed with designs and do the sewing automatically at the push of a button.

You do not have to tack your quilt when using a long-arm machine. Instead, the quilt top and quilt back are pinned to muslin feeders that are attached to the frame's rollers. Wadding is rolled between the two layers, resulting in a completely smooth and pucker-free quilt sandwich.

When you have a large quilting area, it is considerably easier and faster to use a long-arm machine than a conventional sewing machine. There is no struggling to manoeuvre a large quilt through a small home model. Elaborate and detailed quilting patterns are easy to achieve on a long-arm because you move the sewing machine instead of the quilt. This allows you to sew over a greater area, for a longer period, saving time and making it easier on your body.

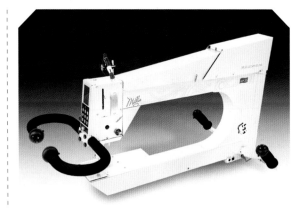

Long-arm quilting machines are large and require a substantial amount of space. Consequently, most home sewers will not have access to a long-arm machine of their own. Instead, they choose to hire a professional long-arm quilter to quilt their project for an hourly rate or for a fee based on the size of the quilt. You can also rent time on long-arm machines at some quilting and sewing stores. This is a great way to experience the ease and speed of long-arm quilting without considerable financial investment.

MAKING STRAIGHT AND CROSS-GRAIN BINDINGS

Once your binding strips are cut, it is time to sew them together. To do so, place two strips right sides together at a 90-degree angle, with the short raw edges overlapping by at least 6 mm (¼ in). Your strips will form an 'L' shape. Draw a diagonal line from the corners on the outside edges of the 'L'. Pin and then sew on the line. Trim the seam to 6 mm (¼ in) and press open. Cut off the small triangles of fabric that extend beyond the raw edges.

TIP

Chain piecing (see page 148) is a fast and effective method to use when sewing many binding strips together.

Top: Giddy quilt by Lydia Rudd.
Below: AMH quilt by Karen Lewis.

SINGLE-FOLD AND DOUBLE-FOLD BINDINGS

All bias, straight or cross-grain bindings can be constructed with a single fold or a double fold. Not to be confused with the pre-packaged bias tapes available at fabric stores, single- and double-fold bindings are specific to quilt making. Which you choose will be determined by the type of project and your own personal preference.

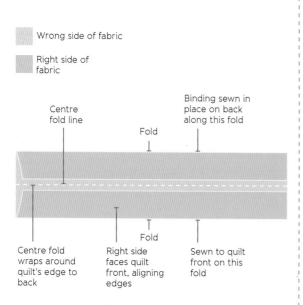

Wrong side of fabric

Right side of fabric

Centre fold line

Fold

Binding sewn in place on back along this fold

Centre fold wraps around quilt's edge to back

Right side faces quilt front, aligning edges

Fold

Sewn to quilt front on this fold

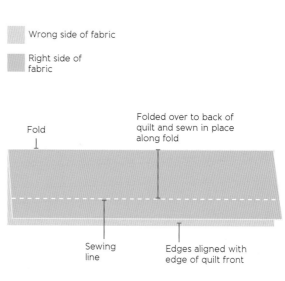

Wrong side of fabric

Right side of fabric

Fold

Folded over to back of quilt and sewn in place along fold

Sewing line

Edges aligned with edge of quilt front

SINGLE-FOLD BINDINGS

Simply put, single-fold bindings are made from one layer of fabric. They are less bulky than double-fold bindings and require less fabric. The single layer of fabric allows for straightforward sewing and easy corner mitres. Single-fold bindings are much weaker than double-fold ones and are best used on wall hangings or other quilts that will not be heavily used or laundered.

DOUBLE-FOLD BINDINGS

'Double fold' indicates that there are two layers of fabric when the binding is sewn to the quilt. Wider binding strips are cut and folded in half lengthways with wrong sides facing. The two raw edges of the binding are aligned with raw edge of the quilt and sewn in place. Although they require more fabric than single-fold bindings, double-fold bindings are thicker, stronger and wear well with heavy use. Their durability makes them the preferred choice of many quilters.

CALCULATING CUTTING WIDTH

The binding width refers to the amount of binding that is seen on the front of the quilt. Traditionally this is 6 mm (¼ in), but it can be any measurement up to 1.8 cm (⅝ in), based on how you would like your quilt to look. This measurement along with the seam allowance is what you need to calculate how wide to cut the binding strips.

To calculate single-fold bindings:
(seam allowance × 2) + (binding width × 2) = width of binding strip

To calculate double-fold bindings:
(seam allowance × 2) + (binding width × 4) = width of binding strip

TIP
Quilts with high-loft waddings or thick fabrics may require slightly wider binding strips.

Top: Single-fold binding.
Bottom: Double-fold binding.

◈ SQUARING THE QUILT AND ATTACHING THE BINDING

Before you can sew the binding to your quilt, make sure that all the edges are straight and the corners are square. Traditionally, the binding is machine sewn to the front of the quilt and then folded over the raw edges and hand sewn to the back.

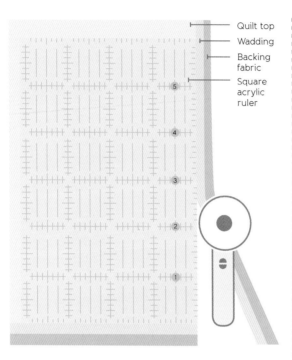

Quilt top
Wadding
Backing fabric
Square acrylic ruler

SQUARING THE QUILT

This is easy to do using a square acrylic ruler, rotary cutter and cutting mat. Simply line up the edges of the ruler with one corner of the quilt and, using the rotary cutter, trim away excess wadding and backing fabric along the length of the ruler. Carefully move the ruler along the side of the quilt, line it up with the edge you just cut and trim the quilt along the ruler's edge. Continue in this manner until the entire quilt is squared.

ATTACHING THE BINDING

Most quilters start binding in the middle of one side of the quilt. It's a good idea to lay the binding around the quilt first to make sure that no seams end up on the corners. If they do, adjust your beginning spot accordingly.

Line up the raw edge of the binding with the raw edge of the quilt. Leaving an 20 cm (8 in) tail, sew the binding to the quilt with 6 mm (¼ in) seam allowance. Begin by backstitching and continue to sew until you reach the first corner.

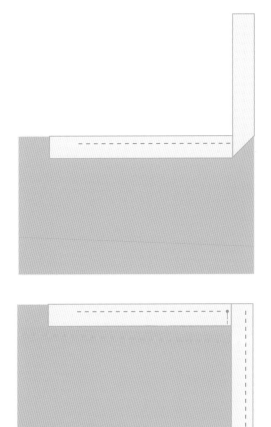

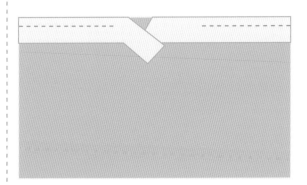

To mitre the corner, stop sewing 6 mm (¼ in) from the corner and backstitch. Lift the presser foot and needle and cut the thread. Rotate the quilt 90 degrees and fold the binding upwards at a 45-degree angle so the raw edge is in line with the side of the quilt you will sew next. Fold the binding back on itself. The fold should rest even with the side of the quilt that you just sewed. Begin sewing the binding to the next side of the quilt 6 mm (¼ in) from the corner. Continue to attach the binding to the quilt, making mitres at all corners as you come to them. Stop sewing when you are 20 cm (8 in) from your starting point and cut the binding, leaving an 20 cm (8 in) tail.

To join the binding ends, lay one tail down across the quilt and cut its end perpendicular to the edge. Lay the second tail over the first and trim it so that the tails overlap by the width of the binding strip. Unfold the bindings and place them right sides together, matching raw edges, at a 90-degree angle to form an 'L'. Draw a diagonal line from the outside edges of the 'L'. Pin the strips together and sew along the line. Make sure the binding is joined correctly and lies flat. If so, trim the seam to 6 mm (¼ in), finger press it open and re-fold the binding. Finally, finish machine sewing the binding to the quilt top.

◈ FINISHING THE BINDING

Once you have attached the binding to the front of the quilt, it is time to sew it to the back. Choose a thread that coordinates with either the binding fabric or the backing fabric, so any noticeable stitches blend in. Cut the thread about 45 cm (18 in) long, thread a hand sewing needle and knot the thread. You can choose to use a single or double strand of thread. A double strand will be stronger, but it may be more visible.

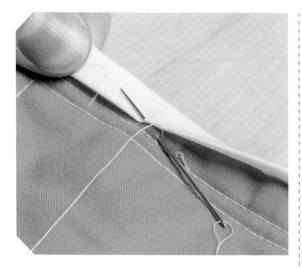

Press the binding towards the back of the quilt to make it flat. Fold it over towards the back, covering the line of machine stitching. You can use pins or clips to keep it in place if you like. Bury your knot in the seam allowance of the quilt. Then, using small and evenly spaced blind or ladder stitches, sew the binding to the back of the quilt. When you come to the corners, fold the mitres neatly on the front and the back.

MACHINE-SEWN BINDINGS
Although attaching a binding by machine and then finishing it by hand is customary, it is also possible to sew the entire binding by machine. This method is certainly faster than hand sewing the binding, but it will often leave noticeable stitches on both sides of the quilt.

There are two ways to sew the binding by machine. The first method is stitching in the ditch. After you have sewn the binding to the front of the quilt, pin the binding to the back of the quilt so it covers the machine stitching. Make sure the pins are oriented so that you can easily pull them out as you come to them while you sew. With the quilt facing up, sew in the ditch next to the binding, catching it on the back.

The other method requires that you attach the binding to the back of the quilt before you sew it to the front of the quilt. Once it is sewn to the back, fold the binding to the front and pin it in place. Sew the binding down by edge stitching it in place with a straight or small zig-zag stitch.

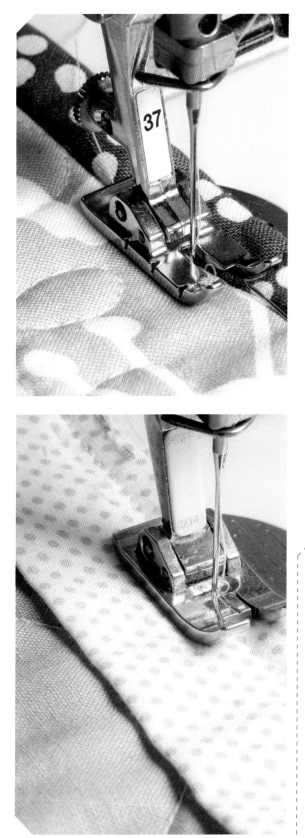

TIP
Using a walking foot to attach the binding will make the layers smooth and easy to manage.

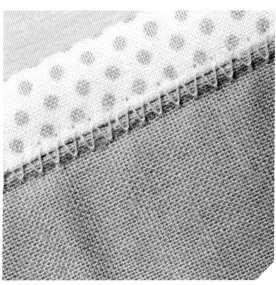

◈ OTHER FINISHING METHODS

While most quilts are finished with a separate, applied binding, there are other methods you can use to complete your quilt. Using the backing as a self-binding and turning the quilt are two alternate ways to create a finished quilt edge. Although these methods are straightforward and easy to achieve, they are not as common or as strong as an applied binding.

SELF-BINDING

In this method, excess backing fabric is trimmed and folded over to the front of the quilt to form a binding. Although finishing your quilt in this manner is simple and quick, not to mention economical, it is not a good choice for all projects. Items that will be heavily used would benefit most from a traditional quilt binding. Also, because it requires a large, flat work surface, this may not be the best choice for large projects or if you are short on space.

To use the backing as binding, make sure the backing fabric is at least 7.5 cm (3 in) larger than the quilt top on all sides. Sandwich, tack and quilt your project. When you have finished quilting, cut the wadding flush with the edges of the quilt top, taking care not to cut through the backing fabric. Determine how much binding will show on the front of the quilt and trim the backing fabric to twice that measurement. Fold the raw edges of the backing so they meet the quilt's edge, and press. Fold again, covering the raw edges. Pin the self-binding in place and sew to the quilt's top using a small blind stitch. To mitre the corners, sew one side down first and then tuck the fabric on the adjoining side under at a 45-degree angle and tack in place.

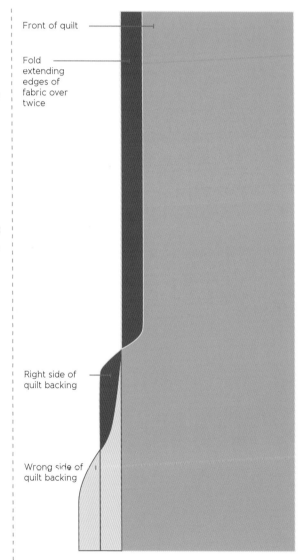

Front of quilt

Fold extending edges of fabric over twice

Right side of quilt backing

Wrong side of quilt backing

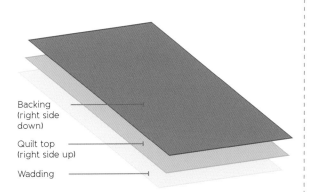

Backing
(right side
down)

Quilt top
(right side up)

Wadding

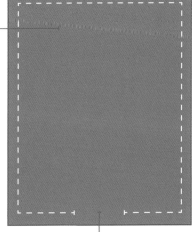

Backing
(wrong
side)

Leave 25 cm (10")
opening for turning

TURNING

Turning a quilt is essentially sewing it together with seams along all four sides with a small hole left to turn it right side out. Also a fast and easy way to finish a quilt, this method works best when tying a quilt.

Cut the wadding and the backing to the same size as the quilt top. Lay the wadding down on a flat surface and smooth it out. Place the quilt top on the wadding with the right side up. Next, lay the backing fabric on the quilt top with its right side down. Pin through all layers along the edges of the quilt sandwich. Using a walking foot, sew the layers together with a 13 mm (½ in) seam allowance, pivoting at the corners. Leave a 25 cm (10 in) gap for turning. Turn the quilt right side out and press the seams allowances of the gap towards the inside of the quilt. Whip stitch the opening closed and tie the quilt as desired.

Quilt front
(right side)

Tuck ends
in and sew
shut with a
whipstitch

Tie
quilt as
desired

ANGELA WALTERS

Angela Walters is well known not just for her quilts, but also for her machine quilting. Her innovative and contemporary quilting style is detailed, expressive and works wonderfully with modern quilts. Using a long-arm machine, she complements her customers' quilt tops with exquisite, modern quilting designs. She chronicles her work on her blog, Quilting is My Therapy, and is the author of two books on free-motion quilting.

Unlike many quilters, Angela did not grow up sewing. She says that she had never set eyes on a sewing machine and did not realise what a quilt was until she was married. In her husband's family, quilts are considered serious business. Both his grandmother and grandfather sewed and always had a project or two going. They loved to construct quilts to give to their family members at the annual family reunion. When Angela and her husband failed to win one of these treasures, Angela bought a stack of fabrics and asked Grandpa for quilting lessons.

Grandpa began by teaching Angela how to cut and sew, starting her on her quilting path. He encouraged her to buy a long-arm quilting machine and gave her quilt tops to practise on. She quickly realised that while piecing a quilt top was nice, it was machine quilting that really made her heart sing.

To develop new quilting designs, Angela draws. She has always been a doodler and keeps a sketchbook to jot down ideas as they come to her. Free drawing keeps her mind fresh and allows Angela to be creative without any particular plan for what the designs should be.

Angela credits her customers and their vision for their quilts as her inspiration. She especially likes working on modern quilts and enhances their designs with the quilting by creating secondary patterns and imagining what the quilt blocks would look like if the lines were extended into the negative space. She prefers a lot of dense quilting, particularly on solid fabrics where the quilting is more evident. Angela chooses thread that blends well so that it does not compete with the quilt top. She tries to honour the quilt's design and says, 'I also like to determine the most important part of the quilt – whether that's the piecing, the fabric, or the pattern – and do everything I can to have the quilting point to that.'

Clockwise from top: Groove, designed and pieced by Emily Cier; Impracticality, pieced by Angela Walters;
Quilting detail on fabric; Raindrops, designed and pieced by Tula Pink; Ditto, designed and pieced by Julie Herman.

PENNY LAYMAN AND KERRY GREEN OF SEW-ICHIGO

The ladies behind the Sew-Ichigo blog are an inspiring duo: they met through an organised online quilting bee. The Ringo Pie Bee, as it was called, focused on paper-pieced quilt blocks, particularly those found in the (out of print) book Patchwork 318 by Kumiko Fujita. Kerry and Penny realised that they shared similar taste in fabrics and had a mutual appreciation of each other's work. They decided to join forces to create a blog and online shop for their original paper-piecing patterns.

Penny began sewing as a child and started her blog, Sewtakeahike, to showcase her home decorating projects. When she first discovered paper piecing, she was amazed at the possibilities that it presented. Inspired by Japanese quilters and their designs, she began perfecting her paper-piecing techniques and designing her own blocks. She prefers to paper piece using a paper foundation and says, 'Designing blocks is very appealing to me because there are so many ways to break a design up into a pattern, so there is no right or wrong, just preferences.'

Kerry was a creative child and attended a school that encouraged sewing. She credits the online sewing community with inspiring her to continue her sewing journey. By joining swaps and developing friendships with like-minded individuals, Kerry found the work of Japanese quilters and began paper piecing soon after. Greaseproof paper piecing is Kerry's preferred way of realising her designs. This technique, while more challenging than foundation paper piecing, allows Kerry to include curves in her designs. She says, 'I love how paper piecing can capture the essence of an object or theme and communicate an era or a feeling with a few simple shapes.'

The cohesive nature of this pair's design sensibilities is evident in everything that they team up to create. Sew-Ichigo's cute, graphic and original designs are inspired by Kerry and Penny's love of retro-inspired imagery and 'kitchenalia'. The twosome likes to develop themed groups of patterns that can be used separately or together. From kitchen appliances to spools of thread and buttons, the paper-piecing patterns are fresh and unique. Additionally, Penny and Kerry strive to make Sew-Ichigo about more than just selling their patterns. The blog is chock-full of various projects, helpful tutorials and paper-piecing tips that provide inspiration and know-how to quilters of all abilities.

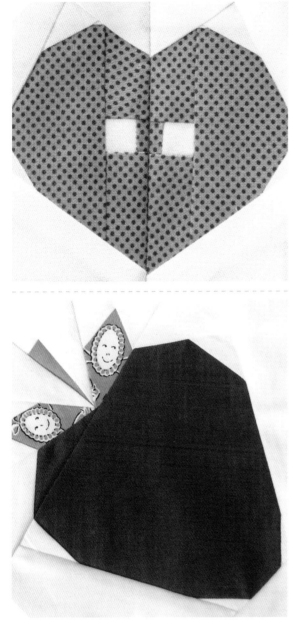

CUP CAKE

Clockwise from top left: Button It Heart; Button It Cupcake;
Kitchen Classics; Strawberry Ichigo.

RESOURCES

GLOSSARY

BACKING
The fabric used for the reverse, or back side, of a quilt.

BASE CLOTH
Plain fabric that is further printed on.

BIAS
The thread line that is at a 45-degree angle to the lengthways and crosswise grains of the fabric.

BINDING
A strip of fabric used to finish a quilt and cover its raw edges.

BLOCK
A single fabric unit, patchwork or otherwise, that is sewn to other similar units to form a quilt top.

BORDER
A band of fabric, plain or pieced, surrounding the quilt along its edges.

CORNERSTONES
Plain or patchwork squares that interrupt a quilt's sashing or borders at the corners.

FABRIC GRAIN
The direction in which a fabric's threads are woven together. Crosswise grain refers to the threads that run perpendicular to the selvedges and lengthways grain refers to the threads that run parallel to the selvedges.

FABRIC WEAVE
The pattern for manufacturing a fabric, as determined by the way the yarns are used to produce different effects and densities.

FABRIC WEIGHT
The lightness or heaviness of a fabric, often calculated by grams per metre. It is also a relative term relating to the thickness and feel of a fabric.

FREE-MOTION QUILTING
A technique in which the sewing machine feed dogs are lowered, allowing the quilt to be moved in any direction under the needle to achieve various designs.

HAND QUILTING
The process of sewing the quilt layers together by hand using a needle and thread with a small running stitch.

LONG-ARM QUILTING
The process in which the quilt top, wadding and backing are attached to a large frame and sewn together using an industrial-strength machine.

NAP
The raised pile of a fabric that runs in one direction. When you run your hand across the fabric, if it feels smooth, it is with the nap. If it is rough, it is against the nap.

PIECING
The process of sewing shapes and blocks together, by hand or with a sewing machine.

PRE-CUTS
Fabric that is purchased cut to a particular size instead of being sold off the bolt.

PREPARED FOR DYEING (PFD)
Fabric that has been pre-washed and pre-treated to accept dyes more easily.

QUILT SANDWICH
The three layers of a quilt. The quilt top is above and the backing is below the middle layer of wadding.

SASHING
Plain or pieced strips of fabric separating blocks in a quilt top.

SELVEDGE
The finished edges of the fabric that keeps it from unravelling.

TACKING
The process by which one fabric is tacked to another with loose, hand-sewn stitches to hold it in place before sewing.

THREAD COUNT
The number of threads woven together in one square inch of fabric.

TYING
The method in which the quilt layers are joined with short lengths of knotted thread or yarn.

WADDING
The insulating middle layer of a quilt.

WARP
The threads of a woven fabric that run parallel to the selvedges and make up the lengthways grain.

WEFT
The threads of a woven fabric that run perpendicular to the selvedges and make up the crosswise grain.

CONTRIBUTORS

PROFILES

Malka Dubrawsky
stitchindye.blogspot.com

Kerry Green
verykerryberry.blogspot.com
sew-ichigo.blogspot.com

Rita Hodge
www.redpepperquilts.com

Anna Maria Horner
www.annamariahorner.com

Penny Layman
sewtakeahike.typepad.com
sew-ichigo.blogspot.com

Blair Stocker
blairpeter.typepad.com

Carrie Strine
carriestrine.squarespace.com

Angela Walters
www.quiltingismytherapy.com

Kajsa Wikman
syko.typepad.com

CONTRIBUTORS

Anita Amodeo
www.margretmarysplace.blogspot.co.uk

Frieda Anderson
www.friestyle.com

APQS
www.apqs.com

Katherine Codega
katherinecodega.tumblr.com
www.etsy.com/shop/KatherineCodega

Sara Cook
www.saracook.co.uk

Joanna Corney
www.joannacorney.co.uk

Meredith Daniel
www.oliviajanehandcrafted.com/blog

Jessica Fincham
www.sewandquilt.co.uk
messyjessecrafts.blogspot.co.uk

Folk Fibers
www.folkfibers.com

Elizabeth Fram
www.elizabethfram.com

Mary Claire Goodwin
www.splendorfallsmc.blogspot.com

Lucrecia Hale
www.forthelovequilts.blogspot.com
www.forthelovedesigns.bigcartel.com

Andi Herman
www.patchandi.com

Stephanie Hill
www.etsy.com/shop/SimplyReverie

Debbie Homick
happylittlecottage.blogspot.uk
www.etsy.com/shop/HappyLittleCottage

Emma How
www.sampaguitaquilts.blogspot.com
www.sampaguitaquilts.etsy.com

Lynn Krawczyk
SmudgedTextilesStudio.com

Cindy Lammon
hyacinthquiltdesigns.blogspot.com

Karen Lewis
www.blueberry-park.co.uk
www.etsy.com/shop/BlueberryPark

Annie London
www.designerstitches.net

Anne Lullie
www.annelullie.com

Clare Mansell
www.flickr.com/claremansell

Leila McCullough
www.flickr.com/photos/26684469@N06

Leslie Keating
www.mazeandvale.com
www.etsy.com/shop/mazeandvale
www.lesliekeating.com

Amanda Jean Nyberg
crazymomquilts.blogspot.com

Heather Pregger
www.heatherquiltz.com

Melissa Robinson
www.clothwork.blogspot.com

Siobhan Rogers
beaspokequilts.blogspot.com.au
www.etsy.com/shop/SiobhanRogers
www.spoonflower.com/profiles/beaspoke
twitter.com/BeaSpokeQuilts

Lydia Rudd
www.etsy.com/shop/DreamPatch
www.dreampatch.com.au

Saké Puppets
sakepuppets.com

Dorie Schwarz
www.tumblingblocks.net

Amy Sinibaldi
www.nanacompany.typepad.com

Lura Schwarz Smith
www.lura-art.com

Sarah Ann Smith
www.sarahannsmith.com

Terri Tester
www.flickr.com/photos/57421358@N08

traceyjay quilts
traceyjayquilts.blogspot.com

Carol Ann Waugh
www.carolannwaugh.com

FURTHER READING

BOOKS

Anna Maria's Needleworks Notebook. Anna Maria Horner. Wiley, 2012

Color Your Cloth: A Quilter's Guide to Dyeing and Patterning Fabric. Malka Dubrawsky. Lark Books, 2009.

Free-Motion Quilting with Angela Walters: Choose & Use Quilting Designs for Modern Quilts. Angela Walters. Stash Books, an imprint of C&T Publishing, 2012.

Fresh Quilting: Fearless Color, Design, and Inspiration. Malka Dubrawsky. Interweave, 2010.

Handmade Beginnings: 24 Sewing Projects to Welcome Baby. Anna Maria Horner. Wiley, 2010.

In The Studio with Angela Walters: Machine-Quilting Design Concepts Add Movement, Contrast, Depth & More. Angela Walters. Stash Books, an imprint of C&T Publishing, 2012.

Liberty Love: 25 Projects to Quilt and Sew Featuring Liberty of London Fabrics. Alexia Marcelle Abegg. Stash Books, an imprint of C&T Publishing, 2012.

Modern Quilts, Traditional Inspirations: 20 New Designs with Historic Roots. Denyse Schmidt. STC Craft/Melanie Falick Book, 2012.

Quilting Modern: Techniques and Projects for Improvisational Quilts. Jacquie Gering and Katie Pedersen. Interweave, 2012

Scandinavian Stitches: 21 Playful Projects with Seasonal Flair. Kajsa Wikman. Stash Books, an imprint of C&T Publishing, 2010.

Seams to Me: 24 New Reasons to Love Sewing. Anna Maria Horner. Wiley, 2008.

Sunday Morning Quilts: 16 Modern Scrap Projects Sort, Store, and Use Every Last Bit of Your Treasured Fabrics. Amanda Jean Nyberg and Cheryl Arkison. C&T Publishing, 2012.

We Love Color: 16 Iconic Quilt Designers Create with Kona (r) Solids. Compiled by Susanne Woods for Stash Books, an imprint of C&T Publishing, 2012.

MAGAZINES

Fat Quarterly
www.fatquarterly.com/

Love Quilting and Patchwork Magazine
www.molliemakes.com

Quilty
www.heyquilty.com/index.html

USEFUL WEBSITES

American Quilter's Society
www.americanquilter.com

Beth Maddocks
piecebynumber.com

Brighton Sewing Centre
www.brightonsewingcentre.co.uk

Charise Randell
charisecreates.blogspot.com

Cloud9 Fabrics
cloud9fabrics.com

Etsy
www.etsy.com

Free Spirit Fabrics
www.freespiritfabric.com

The Modern Quilt Guild
themodernquiltguild.com

Pinterest
pinterest.com

Purl Soho
www.purlsoho.com/purl

QuiltCon
www.quiltcon.com

Quilty Pleasures
www.quilty-pleasures.co.uk

Sew, Mama, Sew
sewmamasew.com

Studio Art Quilt Associates
www.saqa.com

PHOTO CREDITS

Unless otherwise stated here, photographs are by the quilt designer

7: Quilt by Erin Burke Harris Photo by Michael Wicks

14: Reproduction fabrics by Judie Rothermel Photo by Jessica Fincham.

44: Quilt by Sara Cook Photo by Michael Wicks

54: Quilt by Sara Cook Photo by Michael Wicks

60: Left: photo by Emilee Fuss www.emileefuss.com

72: Photo and quilt by Siobhan Rogers

80: Photo and quilt blocks by Jessica Fincham

88: Quilt by Sara Cook. Photo by Michael Wicks

96–97: Photo by Michael Wicks

100: Quilts by Sara Cook. Photo by Michael Wicks

105: Top: Photo by Michael Wicks

108: Photo by Michael Wicks

109: Bottom: Photo by Michael Wicks

110: Both photos by Eric Law eric.law@shootmyart.com

111: Top left and bottom: Photo by Eric Law eric.law@ shootmyart.com

112: Right: photo by Kerby C. Smith

113: Bottom: photo by Kerby C. Smith

115: Top: both photos by Wes Magyar

116: Ruby baby quilt and photo by Debbie Homick

125: Photo by Michael Wicks

128: The Tide is Hire quilt and photo by Sarah Ann Smith

135: Photo by Michael Wicks

139: Photos Christina Carty-Francis and Diane Pederson of C&T Publishing, Inc. © C&T Publishing, Inc.

142: Hansel and Gretel photo and quilt by Amy Sinibaldi

144: Circle of Geese pattern used with permission of Beth Maddocks, Piece By Number

145: Hello Spring pattern used with permission of Charise Randell, Charise Creates

162: Photo by Michael Wicks

170: Photo by Michael Wicks

178: Photo courtesy of APQS

180: Photo by Michael Wicks

INDEX

ACKNOWLEDGEMENTS

Back in the beginning of 2012 I was looking for something to give me purpose. I said it out loud and the universe must have been listening – a week later I received an email from Isheeta Mustafi about this book. A great many thanks to her for giving me this opportunity and for her encouragement and help during the beginning stages of writing this book.

Additional thanks to Jennifer Osborne, Tamsin Richardson and all of the incredible team at RotoVision, along with Amy Marson and Gailen Runge at C&T Publishing, for making Quiltessential the beautiful book that it is. Thanks also to Liz Jones for copy editing the text and to Diane Leyman for the photo research. I'm especially indebted to my editor, Jane Roe, for the answers to my numerous questions, extensive guidance and constant assistance as I got the hang of this book-writing gig. Jane, you made my job easy.

I was privileged to interview an impressive group o f quilters whose quilts inspire me to create more. Thank you to Malka Dubrawsky, Kerry Green, Rita Hodge, Anna Maria Horner, Penny Layman, Blair Stocker, Carrie Strine, Angela Walters and Kajsa Wikman for generously giving your time and sharing your talent with me and my readers. I'm also very appreciative of the numerous quilters who allowed us to showcase photos of their quilts in this book. Thanks to all of you for sharing your work.

I was blessed to have the support of numerous friends as I undertook this project. Huge thanks to Marcia Seiler for not only being my friend and fellow crafter, but also my lawyer and photographer as well. Thanks to Emily Demsky for always listening to me and for her enthusiasm about this book from the start. Caroline Thornewill always has my back and I appreciate that more than she knows. Melissa Frantz and Blair Stocker are the best sounding board a girl could ask for. Thanks to them for brainstorming with me and for cheering me on from afar. I'm also grateful for each member of the Eye Forum for being there for me.

It's unlikely that I would be as enamoured with sewing if it weren't for my parents, Mary Grace and Kevin Burke, and their insistence that I take home-ec in seventh grade. Thank you, Mom and Dad, for all the love, support and encouragement in everything I do. And, thanks too, for buying me my first sewing machine.

Thanks also to my mother-in-law, Jean Harris, for driving me to fabric stores, cutting tiny quilt pieces and always being willing to help me on a project. My biggest thanks to my little family for their unwavering support as I tackled this project. Jane and Kate, you are my sunshine and I feel quite lucky I get to be your mom. I'm thankful for the excitement you have about the things I make and for understanding that sometimes I need it to be quiet when I work.

Thank you, Fatty, for being my best friend and biggest fan. Thank you for loving me and making me laugh. I appreciate your willingness to scout out fabric stores in every city we visit, for understanding when take-out is a necessity, for putting up with my messes and for having the brilliant idea of champagne Tuesday. This one is for you.